Jack the Ripper

Jack the Ripper

New and future titles in the series include:

Alien Abductions

Angels

Atlantis

The Bermuda Triangle

The Curse of King Tut

Dragons

Dreams

ESP

The Extinction of the Dinosaurs

Extraterrestrial Life

Fairies

Fortune-Telling

Ghosts

Haunted Houses

The Kennedy Assassination

King Arthur

Life After Death

The Loch Ness Monster

Pyramids

Stonehenge

UFOs

Unicorns

Vampires

Witches

The Mystery Library

Jack the Ripper

Natalie M. Rosinsky

LUCENT
BOOKS®

THOMSON
———— * ————™
GALE

San Diego • Detroit • New York • San Francisco • Cleveland • New Haven, Conn. • Waterville, Maine • London • Munich

On cover: This dark alley in London's modern-day Whitechapel District was the scene of several murders committed by Jack the Ripper in 1888.

LIBRARY OF CONGRESS CATALOGING-IN-PUBLICATION DATA

Rosinsky, Natalie M. (Natalie Myra)
  Jack the Ripper / by Natalie M. Rosinsky.
    v. cm. — (The mystery library)
Includes bibliographical references and index.
Contents: A case that haunts us—Autumn of terror—"Oh, murder!"—Was the Ripper mad or sane?—Was his motive hatred or love?—Does science have the answer?
  ISBN 1-59018-444-0 (hardback : alk. paper)
  1. Jack the Ripper—Juvenile literature. 2. Serial murders—England—London—History—19th century—Juvenile literature. [1. Jack the Ripper. 2. Serial murderers. 3. Murder—England.] I. Title. II. Series: Mystery library (Lucent Books)
HV6535.G6L6574 2004
364.152'3'092—dc22

2003017761

Printed in the United States of America

Contents

Foreword

In Shakespeare's immortal play, *Hamlet*, the young Danish aristocrat Horatio has clearly been astonished and disconcerted by his encounter with a ghost-like apparition on the castle battlements. "There are more things in heaven and earth," his friend Hamlet assures him, "than are dreamt of in your philosophy."

Many people today would readily agree with Hamlet that the world and the vast universe surrounding it are teeming with wonders and oddities that remain largely outside the realm of present human knowledge or understanding. How did the universe begin? What caused the dinosaurs to become extinct? Was the lost continent of Atlantis a real place or merely legendary? Does a monstrous creature lurk beneath the surface of Scotland's Loch Ness? These are only a few of the intriguing questions that remain unanswered, despite the many great strides made by science in recent centuries.

Lucent Books' Mystery Library series is dedicated to exploring these and other perplexing, sometimes bizarre, and often disturbing or frightening wonders. Each volume in the series presents the best-known tales, incidents, and evidence surrounding the topic in question. Also included are the opinions and theories of scientists and other experts who have attempted to unravel and solve the ongoing mystery. And supplementing this information is a fulsome list of sources for further reading, providing the reader with the means to pursue the topic further.

The Mystery Library will satisfy every young reader's fascination for the unexplained. As one of history's greatest scientists, physicist Albert Einstein, put it:

The most beautiful thing we can experience is the mysterious. It is the source of all true art and science. He to whom this emotion is a stranger, who can no longer wonder and stand rapt in awe, is as good as dead: his eyes are closed.

A Case That Haunts Us

M ore than a hundred years ago, a series of gruesome murders took place in London, England. The victims were prostitutes, attacked in the middle of the night in the poorest of London's East End neighborhoods, Whitechapel. Flyers as well as newspapers spread word of these crimes: "Ghastly Murder in the East-End. Dreadful Mutilation of a Woman."[1] Terror spread throughout the city as police tried to find and arrest the savage killer. There were few witnesses who could provide information. Those who came forward gave conflicting descriptions of a possible suspect. Medical experts who examined the mutilated bodies disagreed about the knife the killer had used. They also debated about whether his removing parts of the victims' bodies meant that the Whitechapel Murderer had himself had medical training.

Hundreds of letters flooded newspaper and police offices, many claiming to contain information about or from the killer. Some letters were signed "Jack the Ripper," and this ghoulish nickname stuck. The hunt for the Ripper, complete with lurid details and drawings of each killing, made daily headlines for months. Still, two British police forces failed to find him. The unsolved case of Jack the Ripper continues to haunt us today.

Lacking an arrest and conviction, this case has become the ultimate whodunnit. Who was the Ripper? More than one hundred people, at one time or another, have been suspected of being this murderer. How many women did he actually kill? Why did the Ripper commit these horrific crimes? According to historian Donald Rumbelow, these "murders, with their nightmarish mutilations, simply went beyond normal comprehension. It was as if the killer wanted to *shock* the whole community, to fling the murders in its face like an hysterical insult."[2] Were these crimes deliberate, or were they the work of a madman? If the murders were deliberate, what was the killer's motive? Without answers to these questions, the mysterious Jack the Ripper has become legendary, what one writer called "a worldwide symbol of terror."[3]

While police abandoned efforts to find the Ripper after several years, the unsolved mysteries of this case obsess people to this day. As historian Philip Sugden notes, "amateur sleuths on three continents still seek final proof of the identity of Jack the Ripper."[4] Some even claim to have found it. The recent release of previously sealed police records and use of new scientific techniques in criminal investigation have increased speculations published in so-called Ripperature, the literature written about the Ripper.

More than one hundred nonfiction books have been written about the case, though not all are well researched or logical. Some theories put forth about the Ripper are easily contradicted by known facts or are highly unlikely. Unfortunately, there is also, as Philip Sugden remarks, "a long history of dishonesty and fraud in Ripper research."[5] Seeking fame or money, some people have lied about clues to these crimes. Today, active Internet websites and three print journals also focus on the Ripper case. Numerous novels, short stories, and even comic books have been written about Jack the Ripper. Strangely, this faceless killer has also been portrayed many times, with many different faces, in films, plays, and episodes of television series. In some people's minds, these fictional images have come to be seen as fact.

In this photo still from the movie From Hell, *an elegantly dressed Jack the Ripper leaves the scene of one of his gruesome murders.*

Films have often shown the Ripper as an elegant, top-hatted gentleman. Moving silently through nighttime fog, he approaches his victim—a young, attractive woman. Suddenly, a knife flashes downward! Evidence collected about the Ripper's crimes shows that such details are false. Even when considering the facts that are known, people disagree about their significance. Has the identity of this brutal serial killer already been discovered? Who are the most likely suspects in this case? The identity of Jack the Ripper remains controversial, one of the greatest mysteries in the history of crime.

Chapter 1

Autumn of Terror

In the autumn of 1888, news of murderous Jack the Ripper spread across Great Britain. While his crimes horrified an entire nation, these murders were committed within a mile of each other, in a grim neighborhood that was already infamous.

The Abyss

Violence and crime were common on the dark, dirty streets of London's East End. It was home to slaughterhouses, rag shops, and slums—a place, one visitor wrote, "where every citizen wears a black eye."[6] Many of its nine hundred thousand inhabitants led lives filled with such noise and chaos that a nighttime cry of "Murder!" could be ignored. Ministers and others who wanted to clean up these slums described them in hellish terms. Andrew Mearns, one of these reformers, wrote:

> Every room in these rotten and reeking tenements [residences] houses a family, often two. In one cellar a sanitary inspector reports finding a father, mother, three children, and four pigs! In another room a missionary found a man ill with small-pox, his wife just recovering from her eighth confinement [pregnancy], and the children running about half naked and covered with dirt. Here are seven people living in one underground kitchen,

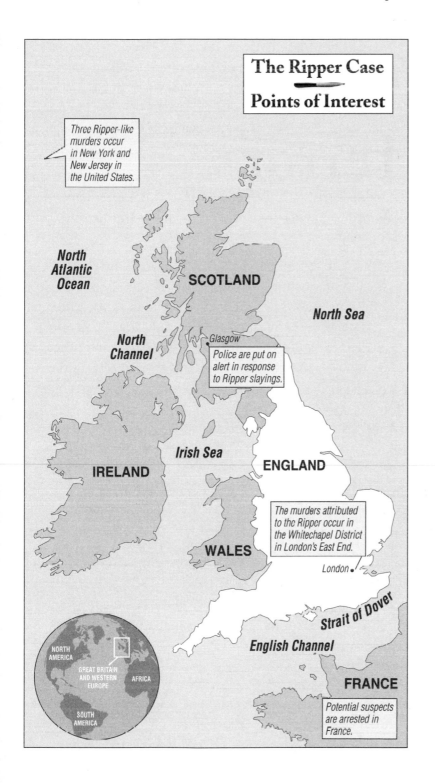

The Ripper Case

Points of Interest

Three Ripper-like murders occur in New York and New Jersey in the United States.

North Atlantic Ocean

SCOTLAND

North Sea

North Channel

Glasgow
Police are put on alert in response to Ripper slayings.

Irish Sea

ENGLAND

IRELAND

The murders attributed to the Ripper occur in the Whitechapel District in London's East End.

WALES

London

NORTH AMERICA

GREAT BRITAIN AND WESTERN EUROPE

AFRICA

SOUTH AMERICA

Strait of Dover

English Channel

FRANCE

Potential suspects are arrested in France.

and a little dead child lying in the same room. Elsewhere is a poor widow, her three children, and a child who had been dead thirteen days. . . . Where there are beds they are simply heaps of dirty rags, shavings or straw, but for the most part these miserable beings find rest only upon the filthy boards. [7]

These were the living conditions of the working poor, who earned so little they could not afford better housing. Sometimes, as Mearns observed, their jobs just added to the dirt and odors of the tenements:

In many cases matters are made worse by the unhealthy occupations followed by those who dwell in these habitations. Here you are choked as you enter by the air laden with particles of the superfluous fur pulled from the skins of rabbits, rats, dogs and other animals in their preparation for the furrier. Here the

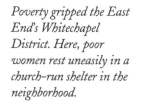

Poverty gripped the East End's Whitechapel District. Here, poor women rest uneasily in a church-run shelter in the neighborhood.

smell of paste and of drying match-boxes, mingling with other sickly odors, overpowers you; or it may be the fragrance of stale fish or vegetables, not sold on the previous day, and kept in the room overnight. Even when it is possible to do so the people seldom open their windows, but if they did it is questionable whether much would be gained, for the external air is scarcely less heavily charged with poison than the atmosphere within. [8]

Within the East End, the Whitechapel District was notorious. Its eighty thousand inhabitants included those without any regular employment, too poor to afford even a room in one of the tenements. Instead, they might sleep outdoors, whole families pressed up against buildings, their clothing caked with mud. As a last resort, someone might enter one of the vermin-ridden workhouses. The government provided these temporary shelters for the homeless in exchange for such hard, unpleasant work as removing hospital waste or carrying rocks. Most people in Whitechapel, though, lived day to day, trying to earn enough money for their next meal or that night's bed (called a "doss") in one of the area's lodging houses.

In 1888, there were more than 230 doss-houses in Whitechapel, where dozens of strangers might sleep next to each other in a room. Whitechapel was also home to more than twelve hundred prostitutes. Many were ill fed, sick, and alcoholic. In the evening they would walk the streets, trying to earn enough money for that night's doss. One writer described these prostitutes as "women with sunken, black-rimmed eyes, whose pallid faces appear and vanish by the light of an occasional gas-lamp, and look so like ill-covered skulls that we start at their stare." [9]

It was on the nighttime streets of Whitechapel, alive with homeless and desperate people caught up in their own misery, that Jack the Ripper struck.

The Whitechapel Murderer

In the early morning hours of August 31, 1888, he killed Mary Ann Nichols. This forty-four-year-old prostitute, often called Polly, had led a hard life. The mother of five grown children, she had already been arrested for being drunk and sleeping outdoors in a public park. Yet a letter she wrote shows that she still felt hopeful. Just four months before her death, Polly Nichols had stopped drinking and worked briefly as a house-cleaner. She wrote then to her father about this job:

> You will be glad to know that I am settled in my new place, and going all right up to now. . . . It is a grand place inside, with trees and gardens back and front. . . . They are very nice people, and I have not too much to do. I hope you are all right and the boy [her son] has got work. So good bye for the present. From yours truly,
>
> Polly.
>
> Anwer soon, please, and let me know how you are.[10]

Polly Nichols did not stay sober, though, and she was soon back on the streets of Whitechapel. Just after 1:00 A.M. on August 31, she cheerfully told an acquaintance, "Never mind! I'll soon get my doss money. See what a jolly bonnet I've got now!"[11] These were Mary Ann Nichols's last known words. Two hours later, a police officer discovered her on a dark street, with—he said—"her throat cut right open from ear to ear . . . lying in a pool of blood . . . the lower part of her person . . . completely ripped open."[12] Nichols's treasured new bonnet lay alongside her.

Police had little information to solve this gruesome killing. Prostitutes had complained about a man mistreating them, someone nicknamed "Leather Apron" because of the garment he wore, used then by butchers and shoemakers. The police eventually found this bad-tempered man, but there was no evidence linking him to the murder. Then, the Ripper struck again.

Leather Apron

On September 8, 1888, he murdered a plump forty-five-year-old woman named Annie Chapman. The mother of three grown children, Chapman had separated years before from her husband. Her drinking had driven them apart. John Chapman continued to give her money, though, until his death in 1886. Annie Chapman then tried to earn her living selling flowers and crocheting. She turned to prostitution when these efforts failed. On September 8, Chapman had complained to friends that she felt feverish and sick. She visited a hospital for medicine, and then reluctantly returned to the crime-ridden streets of Whitechapel to earn money for that night's doss.

At daybreak a horrified workman discovered Chapman's body in the rear yard of a small tenement building. He said: "I saw a female lying down, her clothing up to her knees, and her face covered with blood. . . . What was lying beside her

As described by a contemporary account, a constable discovers the body of Mary Ann Nichols in a pool of blood, the first victim of Jack the Ripper.

I cannot describe—it was part of her body. I did not examine the woman, I was too frightened at the dreadful sight."[13] At Chapman's inquest the coroner who had examined her remains also did not elaborate on her injuries, saying that "further details of the mutilations . . . could only be painful to the feelings of the jury and the public."[14] He did conclude that the precise way in which many of Chapman's internal organs were removed showed that the killer had a knowledge of anatomy. This ghoulish surgery, the coroner went on, must have taken an hour to perform. He also believed that the thin, sharp knife that mutilated Chapman was like those used by some doctors and butchers or slaughterhouse workers.

This information—combined with a folded leather apron found near Chapman's body—caused a frenzy of suspicion in Whitechapel and other East End neighborhoods. Groups of ordinary citizens attacked butchers or leatherworkers they suspected might be the murderous Leather Apron. Police officers, believing the coroner's testimony as important as the

The body of Annie Chapman was discovered in the yard of this bleak tenement house.

cast-off apron, hunted for medical students with a history of mental illness. In their search they also tried to use the testimony of a possible witness. Elizabeth Darrell (sometimes called Elizabeth Long) had been going to market early on the morning of September 8. She reported seeing Annie Chapman with someone she described as a foreign looking man, about five feet two inches tall, wearing a brown deerstalker hat. Because many immigrants lived in the East End, though, describing someone as foreign was not a great help. It only increased any fears or suspicions, however groundless, some people had about immigrants.

"Drunk with Blood"

Newspaper reports also increased people's fears. One report warned readers:

> London lies to-day under the spell of a great terror. A nameless reprobate—half-beast, half-man—is at large, who is daily gratifying his murderous instincts on the most miserable and defenceless classes of the community. . . . The ghoul-like creature who stalks through the streets of London . . . is simply drunk with blood, and he will have more. [15]

Such sensational news sold more copies. Because newspapers did not have hard clues or a trial to write about, historian Perry Curtis comments that they were "forced to fill the gaps with descriptions of conditions in Whitechapel, reports of sightings of suspects and minor attacks on women, suggestions for catching the killer, [and] sharp criticism of the police." [16] Letters to the editor became a popular part of this coverage. Some letters showed their authors' prejudices, with comments that no true Englishman could have committed these crimes. Their writers believed only an Asian or Jewish immigrant could be the killer. They noted that many Jewish immigrants lived in the East End. Other letters came from disturbed people claiming to be the murderer himself.

On September 17, 1888, editors at the Central News Agency received one such handwritten, misspelled, and poorly punctuated letter, the first ever to be signed "Jack the Ripper." Its author mentioned George Lusk, an East End businessman who had organized a community group to hunt the killer on their streets. The letter writer laughed at this group, boasted that *he* was watching *them*, and gleefully threatened to kill again. The letter said:

> Dear Boss
>
> So now they say I am a Yid [Jew] when will they learn Dear old Boss? You and me know the truth dont we. Lusk can look forever hell never find me but I am rite under his nose all the time. I watch them looking for me and it gives me fits ha ha I love my work an I shant stop until I get buckled [caught] and even then watch out for your old pal Jacky.
>
> Catch me if you Can
>
> Jack the Ripper
>
> Sorry about the blood still messy from the last one. What a pretty necklace I gave her.[17]

Police thought this brutal, gloating letter might be from the actual Ripper. At Annie Chapman's inquest, the coroner had not described the way Chapman's severed intestines had been placed across her throat. The necklace mentioned here seemed like a reference to this little-known detail.

On September 25, 1888, another handwritten letter from someone claiming to be Jack the Ripper was sent to the Central News Agency. Gruesomely, its author explained that he was using red ink because the blood he had saved to use had become too thick. This letter writer appeared to take sick pleasure in the crimes he had perpetrated as well as those he planned to commit:

> Dear Boss,
>
> I keep on hearing the police have caught me but they won't fix me just yet. I have laughed when they look

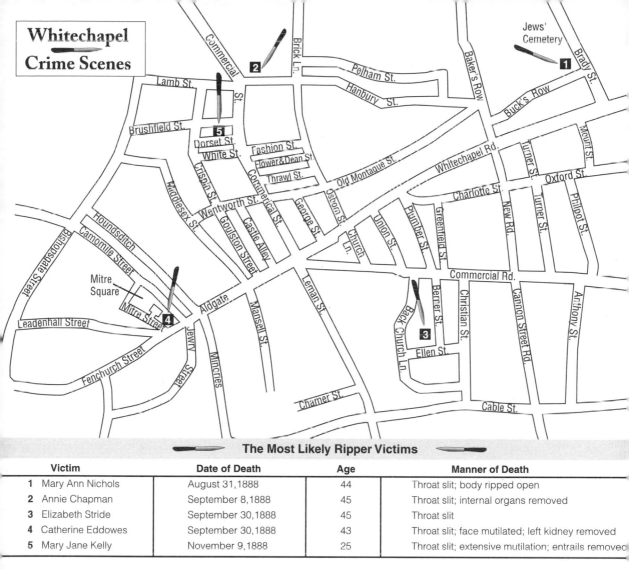

Whitechapel
Crime Scenes

The Most Likely Ripper Victims

	Victim	Date of Death	Age	Manner of Death
1	Mary Ann Nichols	August 31, 1888	44	Throat slit; body ripped open
2	Annie Chapman	September 8, 1888	45	Throat slit; internal organs removed
3	Elizabeth Stride	September 30, 1888	45	Throat slit
4	Catherine Eddowes	September 30, 1888	43	Throat slit; face mutilated; left kidney removed
5	Mary Jane Kelly	November 9, 1888	25	Throat slit; extensive mutilation; entrails removed

so clever and talk about being on the right track. That joke about Leather Apron gave me real fits. I am down on whores and I shan't quit ripping them till I do get buckled. Grand work the last job was. I gave the lady no time to squeal. How can they catch me now. I love my work and want to start again. You will soon hear of me with my funny little games. I saved some of the proper red stuff [blood] in a ginger beer bottle over the last job to write with but it went thick like glue and I can't use it. Red ink is fit enough I hope ha ha. The next job I shall clip the ladys ears off and send to the police officers just for jolly. . . . Keep this letter back til I do a bit more work, then give it out straight. My knife's so nice and sharp I want to get to work right away if I get a chance.

Another taunting message scribbled down the side of this letter read: "Wasnt good enough to post this before I got all the red ink off my hands curse it. No luck yet. They say I'm a doctor now ha ha."[18]

This letter was first published in the *London Daily News* on October 1, 1888. That day, horrified Londoners also learned from headlines that the bloodthirsty Ripper had struck again—twice in one night!

"Some of Us Will Be Killed Next!"

On September 30, 1888, at about 1:00 A.M., a salesman returning to his Whitechapel home discovered the still-warm body of Elizabeth Stride. She lay close to the wall of the building. At first, he could not tell if she was drunk or dead, but then he saw all the blood. As the doctor called to the scene later testified: "The blood was running down the gutter into the drain. . . . There was about a pound of clotted blood close by the body, and a stream all the way from there to the back door of the [building]."[19] Forty-five-year-old Elizabeth Stride had had her throat slit ear to ear.

Swedish immigrant Elizabeth Stride, born Elizabeth Gustafsdotter, had a long history of drunkeness and prostitution. During that autumn of terror, this scarred woman with a mouthful of missing and broken teeth knew that she was at risk. Her fears were documented by Dr. Thomas Barnardo, a physician who tried to help the poor in Whitechapel. He viewed Elizabeth Stride's body in the morgue and identified her as one of a group of prostitutes he had just visited on September 26. All were "thoroughly frightened," he wrote, and one had even "cried bitterly: No one cares what becomes of us. Perhaps some of us will be killed next!"[20] In a further effort to alert the citizens of Whitechapel, Barnardo repeated these prophetic words in a letter to the London *Times*.

Several people may have glimpsed the Ripper with Elizabeth Stride. They gave conflicting descriptions of this suspect. William Marshall, who lived across the street from the crime scene, said that at 11:45 that night he had seen Stride kissing a middle aged man. Fruit seller Matthew Packer believed that, about midnight, he had sold grapes to Stride and a man about five feet seven inches tall who was dressed like a clerk. The police officer who patrolled that part of Whitechapel testified that about 12:30 A.M. he had seen Stride with a clean-shaven man about twenty-eight years old who wore a deerstalker cap and carried a newspaper-wrapped

A Police Gazette *features a drawing of the Ripper attacking a woman with a knife. The ghastly nature of his crimes horrified the nation.*

package. Fanny Mortimer, a resident on the street where Stride was killed, claimed to have seen a man hurrying away with a shiny black bag between 12:30 and 1:00 A.M. Israel Schwartz, who identified Elizabeth Stride's body at the morgue, said that between 12:45 and 1:00 A.M. he had seen her struggle with a man about thirty years old, five feet five inches tall, with dark hair, a mustache, and a peaked cap. Unlike the person Fanny Mortimer saw, he carried nothing in his hands.

While these conflicting descriptions did not help police in their hunt for the Ripper, they did seem to explain why Elizabeth Stride's body was not mutilated. Having so many people nearby had prevented the killer from lingering to commit his brutal version of surgery. Criminologist John Douglas believes that the Ripper's appetite for blood was not satisfied, and so he went on to kill again that night.

"Just for Jolly"

At 1:45 that morning, just a quarter mile away from Elizabeth Stride's body, a cry rang out in Mitre Square. A shocked City of London policeman was calling for help. He shouted, "For God's sake man come out and assist me; another woman has been ripped open!"[21] Constable Watkins had discovered the mutilated corpse of Catherine Eddowes.

Eddowes, a forty-three-year-old mother of grown children, was an alcoholic who was painfully aware of what her drunkeness had cost her. According to one of her married sisters, Eddowes would cry when they met and say, "I wish I was like you."[22] On September 30, Catherine Eddowes had been arrested for sleeping drunkenly in the street. She was just sober enough to be released from jail shortly before 1:00 A.M. Her freedom quickly brought her death.

According to the coroner's report, Eddowes's mutilation and dismemberment were the most savage yet committed by the Ripper. It even appeared that he had tried—as the letter

Catherine Eddowes was discovered with her throat slit, her face mutiliated, and her entrails removed.

written on September 25 threatened—to cut off his victim's ears to mail to the police as a gruesome joke. The official report noted that there was

> great disfigurement of the face, the throat cut across. . . . The abdomen was all exposed. The intestines were drawn out to a large extent and placed over the right shoulder. . . . A piece of about 2 feet was quite detached from the body and laced between the body and the left arm, apparently by design. The lobe and auricle of the right ear was cut obliquely through. . . .

When the body arrived at [the morgue] . . . the clothes were taken off carefully from the body [and] a piece of the deceased's ear fell from the clothing. [23]

One of the victim's organs was missing. The coroner noted that "the left kidney [was] carefully taken out and removed—the left renal artery cut through." [24] The remaining kidney showed Bright's disease, common in alcoholics. From the depth and position of all these cuts, the coroner concluded that Catherine Eddowes's killer had slashed upward as he knelt alongside her.

Other evidence of this murder was found a short distance away from Eddowes's body. Part of a bloody cloth apron, matching the shabby clothes Eddowes was wearing, was discovered on a nearby street. Above the apron, scrawled in chalk on a brick wall, was a mysterious piece of graffiti. Its ungrammatical message was, "The Juwes are the men that will not be blamed for nothing." [25] It was not clear when this message had been written or what, if anything, its connection to the Ripper might be. Yet the commissioner of the Metropolitan Police Force, Sir Charles Warren, ordered it erased. He wanted to prevent a possible riot. Warren feared that alarmed East Enders, seeing this message and thinking it accused a Jew of the Ripper killings, would attack their Jewish neighbors.

Police Commissioner Warren's fears had merit. Even without the mysterious message about "Juwes," some East Enders did turn on their Jewish neighbors, who were at times also known as Hebrews. One newspaper article on October 15, 1888, noted:

The crowds who assembled in the streets began to assume a very threatening attitude towards the Hebrew population of the District. It was repeatedly asserted that no Englishman could have perpetrated such a horrible crime . . . and that it must have been done by a Jew—and forthwith the crowds began to threaten and abuse each of the unfortunate Hebrews they found in the streets."[26]

Rumors and speculations continued. This horrific state of affairs worsened with the news of another, all-too-believable communication from the Ripper.

"From Hell"

On October 16, 1888, George Lusk, already mentioned in one Ripper letter, received a letter and package. The dreadful contents of both suggested they came from the real Jack the Ripper. This letter said it was written "From hell," a location that described both the terror East Enders were feeling that autumn and, possibly, the confusion and anger of its writer, who had enclosed part of a human kidney in the package! This handwritten letter gloated about the mutilation of Catherine Eddowes and promised more to come. It read:

> From hell
>
> Mr. Lusk
>
> Sor,
> I send you half the Kidne I took from one women prasarved it for you tother [the other] piece I fried and ate it was very nise I may send you the bloody knif that took it out if only you wate a while longer
>
> signed Catch me when
> you can
>
> Mishter Lusk.[27]

Most police believed this gruesome letter and memento came from the real Ripper because the kidney—like the other one still inside Catherine Eddowes—showed signs of Bright's disease. Even more conclusively, the packaged kidney was attached to one inch of renal artery. Two inches had remained inside Eddowes's corpse, and the typical length of this artery was three inches. Londoners wondered when and where this monstrous killer would strike next.

For over a month, residents of London lived in dreadful suspense. Newspapers continued to headline, even mock, the police's failure to find the Ripper. Some East Enders banded together in groups to patrol the streets and asked government officials to offer a reward for the Ripper's capture. These so-called vigilance committees did not succeed. In the early morning hours of November 9, 1888, a faint cry was heard in Miller's Court, just off Whitechapel's Dorset Street. Horribly, the wait for the next killing was over.

Chapter 2

"Oh, Murder!"

With this next victim, the Ripper seemed to change some of his habits. For the first time, he chose to attack a young, attractive woman, and he did so indoors. What had not changed was the savage brutality of his crime.

"Plucked from My Mother's Grave"

November 9, 1888, was the last day of Mary Jane Kelly's life. This twenty-five-year-old Irish woman had been a domestic servant who married at sixteen and possibly had a child. When she moved to London in 1884, the blonde, blue-eyed Kelly first worked as a prostitute in fancy areas of the city. By 1887, she was renting a room in the dismal East End. There, Kelly's fresh complexion, bright smile, and slender figure set her apart from the neighborhood's other, bedraggled women. For more than a year, she shared lodgings with a market worker named Joseph Barnett. He had moved out after a recent quarrel.

Between midnight and 1:00 A.M. that morning, several people said they heard Kelly singing as she walked the streets. They recognized the popular, sentimental song, "Only a Violet I Plucked from My Mother's Grave." At about 2:00 A.M., an acquaintance named George Hutchinson twice saw Kelly walking and talking with a man. He heard her tell the man, "Come along, you will be comfortable." Hutchinson heard this man reply in refined, unaccented English. By 3:45 A.M., Kelly was at home. This is when three neighbors or visitors on her block heard a faint cry of "Oh, murder!"[28] coming from her building. In the grim neighborhood of Whitechapel, though, these words—especially if not shouted—were easy to ignore.

Mary Jane Kelly was killed and mutilated in her own home. The privacy of Kelly's home gave Jack the Ripper time to satisfy his blood lust. Her body was mutilated more savagely than any of the other victims. When the landlord, John McCarthy, came at 11:00 A.M. to collect the rent, the door was locked. Peering through a window, he discovered a sight he said he could "never forget . . . if he lived to be a hundred." According to McCarthy:

> She had been completely disembowelled, and her entrails had been taken out and placed upon the table. . . . The woman's nose had been cut off, and her face gashed and mutilated so that she was quite beyond recognition. Both her breasts too had been cut clean away and placed by the side of her liver and other entrails on the table. . . . The body was, of course, covered with blood, and so was the bed.[29]

The coroner's reports gave more precise details of this butchery, but Joseph Barnett's stuttering testimony perhaps better summed up the extent of this massive mutilation. Speaking of his formal identification of Mary Kelly, the woman he had lived with for more than a year, Barnett said only, "I have seen the body, and I identify it by the hair and eyes which is all that I recognize."[30]

"Monsters in Human Shape"

The Whitechapel murders were a constant topic of conversation. Jack the Ripper's horrible crimes were even talked about in church. One minister prayed with his congregation, "God . . . grant that we may hear no more of such deeds . . . and let not monsters in human shape escape."[31] People's fears were increased by the uncertainty of how many women the Ripper had actually killed. There had been violent attacks and murders of women in Whitechapel before Mary Ann Nichols's

This photo of Mary Kelly's lodging house was taken the day after her murder. Her landlord discovered the body when he peered through a broken window (arrow).

death that autumn. Was the Ripper responsible for the brutal attack on Emma Smith the preceding April? Had he savagely killed Martha Tabram on August 7, 1888? Each of these crimes had included knifing and mutilation of the victim's sexual organs. Or, was there more than one "monster in human shape" stalking those dark and dirty streets?

At the time, most police officers believed the Ripper had claimed five lives. These victims were Mary Ann Nichols, Annie Chapman, Elizabeth Stride, Catherine Eddowes, and Mary Jane Kelly. Yet there was some disagreement even about these five. At Elizabeth Stride's inquest, the coroner testified that she had been killed with a shorter knife than the other women. This difference in weapons might mean different killers had committed the murders. A few people also believed that the indoor slaying of Mary Jane Kelly, so unlike the outdoor deaths of the other victims, indicated a murderer other than the Ripper. Even the detectives directly responsible for solving these crimes questioned the number of victims involved. One believed that Jack the Ripper had "killed six victims," while another believed "there were five murders," and a third detective "felt that only four killings could be attributed to the Whitechapel Murderer."[32] When, in the autumn of 1888, police began to hunt for a brutal serial killer, their job was made more difficult because of the uncertainty about how many crimes to include in the investigation.

The investigation was also hampered by the limited tools then available to detectives. The science of fingerprinting was not in wide use, and differences in human blood types were unknown. This is why the untouched scene of Kelly's slaughter did not provide useful evidence about her killer. The police needed more obvious clues, eyewitness accounts, and other leading information to identify and arrest a suspect. Hunting the Ripper, police called upon the citizens of Whitechapel for help.

"To Whom Suspicion Is Attached"

More than eight thousand handbills were printed and distributed throughout the area. They read:

On the mornings of Friday, 31st August, [of] Saturday 8th [September], of Sunday 30 September, 1888, Women were murdered in or near Whitechapel, sup-

posed by someone residing in the immediate neighborhood. Should you know of any person to whom
suspicion is attached, you are earnestly requested to
communicate at once with the Metropolitan Police
Office, 30th September, 1888. [33]

Soon information flooded police offices. Because the
Ripper had left few identifying clues at the crime scenes,
investigators felt they had to give attention to all suggestions,
even those which—as one senior official wrote—"in any ordinary case would be dismissed unnoticed. . . . No hint of any
kind, which was not obviously absurd, [could be] neglected." [34]
These included false accusations and even false confessions
by disturbed individuals.

One man—Robert Donston Stephenson, who sometimes
called himself Dr. Roslyn D'Onston—fit into both categories.
At first, when he contacted newspapers and police, Stephenson
accused a London doctor of being the Ripper. A doctor might
have carried the black bag one witness saw the night Elizabeth
Stride was murdered. This accusation also fit with some coroners' views that the Ripper had medical training. Later,
Stephenson confessed to others that he himself was the Ripper.
Although police were skeptical, they did bring Stephenson in
for questioning. This Ripper-obsessed person, like other false-
ly confessed or accused suspects, was quickly released.

Another unsuccessful attempt to catch the Ripper involved
a house-to-house search of Whitechapel. One resident of
Spelman Street, annoyed by this inconvenience, described it
to a London reporter:

I came home from work yesterday, and as soon as I
opened the front door, two men came up and said, "Do
you live in this front room?" "Yes," I said. "We want to
have a look at it?" "Who are you, and what do you want?"
"We are police officers, and we have come to look for
the murderer." "Do you think I keep the murderer here,
or do you suggest that I associate with him?" I replied.

SLADE WALK

In the 1944 film The Lodger, *the Ripper carries a doctor's bag. A witness in the actual Ripper case reported seeing the killer carrying such a bag.*

They answered that it was their duty to inspect the rooms. I showed them into my room. They looked under the bed, and asked me to open the cupboards. I opened a small cupboard, where I keep plates and things. It is not more than 2 feet wide and about 1 foot in depth. They made an inspection of that also. "Do you think," I said, "that it is possible for a man, or even a child, to be hidden in that small place?" They made no answer, and walked out. Then they went next door and inspected those premises. [35]

While some officers searched the bleak houses of Whitechapel for over a week, others continued to investigate the many butchers and slaughterhouses in the East End. These efforts to locate the Ripper among any mentally unstable or otherwise suspicious workers there were equally futile. Because some witnesses had described the Ripper as foreign, men with unusual accents were also questioned. Innocent Dutch and American tourists found themselves briefly detained in London police stations. Even being overheard talking about the Ripper was sometimes reason enough to be questioned by an officer. The ongoing failure of police to come up with any likely suspects became daily news.

"Catch Whom You May"

Newspaper articles and cartoons mocked police efforts to catch the Ripper. One cartoon suggested that their manhunt for this killer was no more effective than a game of blindman's bluff. The cartoon portrayed a blindfolded officer reaching out to grab whichever person was nearest him, playing a children's game then also known as "catch whom you may."

One scheme to catch the Ripper was the focus of particularly sharp ridicule. After the double slaying of Elizabeth Stride and Catherine Eddowes, bloodhound owners throughout England had offered their dogs to sniff out the Ripper. Even police officers were dismayed when Police Commissioner Warren accepted one of these offers. They realized that the foul odors of Whitechapel would greatly limit the dogs' tracking ability. Warren did not. He began to work with the dogs in a London park, using himself as their target. Newspaper articles mocked the commissioner's escapades with these champion trackers, named Burgho and Barnaby.

The scheme to use bloodhounds not only drew criticism but also delayed the Ripper investigation. Under orders from Warren, police waited for the arrival of these hounds before entering the blood-drenched Kelly crime site, which they, like her landlord, could see through a window. Only after three hours had passed did the waiting officers receive word that Warren's borrowed bloodhounds supposedly had run away. A London *Star* editorial snidely suggested that "these animals . . . finding that they could not get on with the Chief Commissioner . . . resigned."[36]

Mocking the unsuccessful police investigation of the Ripper crimes, a cartoon depicts a bewildered policeman in a game of blind man's bluff.

Comments such as this reflected the resentment felt by the press. Many reporters and editors were dismayed with official police policies toward them during the Ripper case. Officers were instructed not to give interviews to the press and to withhold as many details as possible about each murder. Without hard facts on which to focus, newspapers turned to mocking or sensational pieces such as the bloodhound articles. They printed editorials criticizing the rapid turnover of senior officials in charge of the case. One policeman later wrote that he had "always thought that the higher police authorities in ignoring the power of the Press deliberately flouted a great potential ally, and indeed might have turned that ally into any enemy."[37] In fact, some press activities likely did interfere with efforts to catch the dreaded Ripper.

"This Ghastly Production"

Eager reporters—knowing they would not willingly be given details—followed detectives throughout the East End. Police Commissioner Warren complained that this press "practice impedes the usefulness of detective investigation and moreover keeps alive the excitement in the district and elsewhere."[38] Unscrupulous reporters may even have committed fraud, manufacturing so-called news to report. Of the more than three hundred letters supposedly written by Jack the Ripper, only three or four were finally considered authentic. Some of the rest were thought to have been written by attention seekers, but many were probably penned by reporters themselves. Sir Melville McNaughten, who became assistant chief commissioner of police, later wrote that, because a number of these letters used the same slang expressions, he thought they were authored by the same reporter. McNaughten wrote:

> In this ghastly production I have always thought I could discern the stained forefinger of the journalist—indeed, a year later I had shrewd suspicions as to the

actual author! But whoever did pen the gruesome stuff, it is certain to my mind that it was not the mad miscreant [wrongdoer] who had committed the murders.[39]

In a letter, Chief Inspector John George Littlechild named the two people he and others thought responsible for most of this fraud: a reporter named Tom Bullen of the Central News Agency and his editor, Mr. Moore. Yet at the time, the public was unaware of this probable deception. In their alarm, ordinary citizens added to the pressures felt by police.

People wrote directly to the police and to newspapers with suggestions for catching the Ripper. These included disguising officers as women, armor plating collars to make them knife proof, and even building "mechanical mantraps in female form, whose spring-loaded arms [would] seize the suspect while the machine declare[d] its triumph by loud blasts on a police whistle!"[40] Queen Victoria herself followed the case and offered her own advice. In a letter bearing the royal crest, she wrote:

> The Queen fears that the detective department is not so efficient as it might be. No doubt the recent murders in Whitechapel were committed in circumstances which made detection very difficult; still, the Queen thinks that, in the small area where these horrible crimes have been perpetuated, a great number of detectives might be employed. . . .
>
> Have the cattle boats and passenger boats been examined? Has any investigation been made as to the number of single men occupying rooms to themselves? The murderer's clothes must be saturated with blood and kept somewhere. Is there sufficient surveillance at night?
>
> These are some of the questions that occur to the Queen on reading the accounts of these horrible crimes.[41]

6 Oct 1888

You though your self very clever I reckon when you informed the police But you made a mistake, if you though I dident see you Now I know you know me and I see your little game, and I mean to finish you and send your ears to your wife if you show this to the police or help them if you do I will finish you. It no use your trying to get out of my way Because I have you when you dont expect it and I keep my word as you soon see and rip you up Yours truly Jack the Ripper

You see I know your address.

One of many letters the Ripper is purported to have sent to the police is pictured here. Only a handful of them were thought to be authentic.

This royal interest intensifed government pressure on the police. High-ranking British officials wanted the Ripper found not only to end his horrible crimes but to silence rumors. At home and abroad, people had begun to wonder if there was some hidden conspiracy behind the failure to catch this brutal murderer.

"Person or Persons Unknown"

The Metropolitan Police Force, responsible for most of London, had refused to offer a reward for information about the Ripper. Did its officials have a reason for not wanting the killer found? Perhaps the police were trying to cover up the crimes of a highly placed person. There was even gossip that Jack was a member of the British Parliament's House of Lords. This rumor was widespread enough that it was mentioned in a daily newspaper, which reported:

> There is not the slightest "Truth" [that Prime Minister]
> Lord Salisbury concealed Jack the Ripper . . . on the

night of the last Whitechapel Murder, or that the Home Secretary has instructed [Police Commissioner] Monroe to discontinue all further inquiries into the atrocities in consequence of it having been discovered that Jack is a member of the House of Lords. . . . Some such story was for a long time in circulation at the East End, where [it was] heard more than once that police had received orders to drop the inquiry from high official quarters. [42]

Some East Enders had a simpler explanation for the Metropolitan Police's decision. According to the jury foreman at Polly Nichols's inquest, "If it had been a rich person that was murdered there would have been a reward of 1000 pounds [about 5,000 dollars then] offered, but as it was only a poor unfortunate hardly any notice was taken." [43] This plainspoken workman went on to offer his own reward of 25 pounds (about 125 dollars then) for the Ripper's capture.

In part to end public suspicions, the British government offered to pardon any accomplices who might have information about the killer. On streets and in police stations this notice appeared:

PARDON OFFERED

MURDERER PARDON: Whereas, on November 8 or 9th in Miller's Court, Dorset Street, Spitalfields, Mary Jane Kelly was murdered by person or persons unknown, the Secretary of State will advise the grant of Her Majesty's gracious Pardon to any accomplice, not being a person who contrived or actually committed the Murder, who shall give such information as shall lead to the discovery and conviction of the person or persons who committed the Murder. [44]

This offer of a pardon removed some doubts about possible cover-ups by the Metropolitan Police. Suspicions were further calmed when the smaller City of London police force—with its jurisdiction over the city's central mile in which Catherine Eddowes had been slain—did offer its own reward for information. Yet neither the possibility of a pardon nor the prospect of rewards (offered as well by two newspapers, a legislator, and the largest vigilance committee) produced information that led to the Ripper. This elusive killer began to take on larger-than-life proportions. His power to strike seemed inescapable, like a nightmare that without warning could invade anyone's sleep.

Queen Victoria offered a pardon to any accomplice of the Ripper who provided information leading to his arrest and conviction.

"Take Away His Knife"

In an attempt to cope with this ever present threat, East End children sang skipping rhymes about the Ripper, and their parents bought penny-a-sheet rhymes (called broadsides) that mocked him and their own fears. One such broadside had this to say to readers:

> Has anyone seen him, can you tell us where he is, If you meet him you must take away his knife, Then give him to the women, they'll spoil his pretty fizz [face], And I wouldn't give him twopence for his life.
>
> Now at night when you're undressed and about to go to rest Just you see that he ain't underneath the bed If he is you mustn't shout but politely drag him out And with your poker [iron rod] tap him on the head. [45]

It is significant that, in this rhyme, it is not the police but ordinary people who are considered likely to catch the Ripper. Soon after the slaughter of Mary Jane Kelly, some East Enders were already doubtful about officials' being able to find and arrest her killer.

The hunt for Jack the Ripper spread beyond London. Police were put on the alert in the large city of Glasgow, Scotland. Based on sketches drawn according to one eyewitness account, potential suspects were arrested in France. Newspapers in the United States also warned that this killer had possibly crossed the Atlantic. Three Ripper-like slayings of women took place in New York and New Jersey in 1891 and 1892. The leads proved fruitless, and a definite connection to Jack the Ripper could not be found. Yet each time a woman was brutally slain, her body mutilated on a dark city street, investigators continued to wonder if Jack the Ripper was responsible.

In London in particular, police questioned whether the Ripper slaughtered Rose Mylett in December 1888. Had he returned in 1889 to kill Elizabeth Jackson and Alice

Despite the lack of evidence linking the Ripper to the crime, police speculated that he may have killed Alice McKenzie (pictured).

McKenzie? Finally, was the Ripper responsible in 1891 for the brutal murder of Frances Coles? The victims, crime sites, and—to some extent—mutilations in these cases resembled the five deaths attributed to the Whitechapel Murderer, yet there was no direct evidence linking these later cases to the Ripper. Instead, once again, expert witnesses disagreed about the surgical or anatomical knowledge possessed by the killer.

This lengthening list of possible Ripper victims made it even more difficult to identify and arrest a suspect.

While the official, active London investigation of the Ripper ended with the unsolved slaying of Frances Coles in 1891, police and newspapers continued to receive letters signed "Jack the Ripper" through 1896. Each of these messages claimed responsibility for another, new mutilation and murder or threatened some brutal crime. The messages kept people's fears alive. Was Jack the Ripper lurking around some dark corner? Where and when might he strike next? Whom would he attack? Without knowing the reasons for his terrible deeds, no one could feel truly safe. What could motivate someone not only to kill but mutilate victims so viciously? Fear and a kind of dreadful curiosity led people to speculate about why the Ripper had killed as he did. Their ideas led to many different theories about the identity of this mysterious, monstrous criminal.

Chapter 3

Was the Ripper Mad or Sane?

To this day, the question of Jack the Ripper's sanity remains an unsolved mystery. Some people believe that no sane person could have committed the Ripper's brutal deeds. They say that only a madman—lacking all reason or logical motives—could have possibly killed and mutilated as the Whitechapel Murderer did. This view has been held by amateur as well as official investigators of the case. Others contend that the murders were committed as part of a calculated and deliberate plan.

"Committed by a Lunatic"

One very vocal, early proponent of the madman theory was Dr. L. Forbes Winslow, a specialist in nervous diseases whose family also owned and operated insane asylums. In an 1888 letter to the London *Times*, Winslow wrote:

> I think the murderer is . . . of the upper class of society . . . [and] that the murders have been committed by a lunatic lately discharged from some asylum, or by one who has escaped. If the former, doubtless one who, though suffering from the effects of homicidal mania, is apparently sane on the surface, and consequently

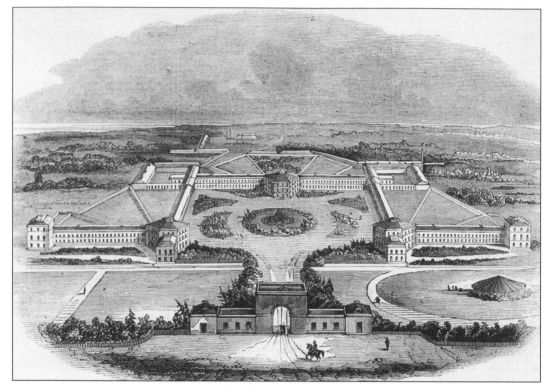

Some investigators felt that the Ripper was insane and may have spent time in a London mental asylum like the one pictured here.

has been liberated, and is following out the inclinations of his morbid imaginations by wholesale homicide. I think the advice given by me a sound one—to apply for an immediate return [of information] from all asylums who have discharged such individuals, with a view of acertaining their whereabouts. [46]

Winslow wrote and, in later years, lectured so often about Jack the Ripper that he became known in the press as the "English Sherlock Holmes of these East End murders." [47] His belief that the Ripper had had medical training also influenced the way this killer was later depicted as a gentleman doctor in some books and movies. Superficially sane, this debonaire character only reveals his madness at the moment he draws his death-dealing knife.

Winslow's intense interest in the Whitechapel Murderer may have led this amateur detective to commit fraud. He claimed to have received a revealing letter from the Ripper before Mary Kelly's murder. Later examination of this letter, whatever its true source, showed that its date had been changed. Winslow was so obsessed with the Ripper that he falsified this personal connection to the case.

Like Winslow, many high-ranking officers believed that madness was the only explanation for these horrific crimes. Their first suspects, then, were not upper-class doctors, who would have seemed out of place in impoverished Whitechapel, but the mentally ill already living in or near its slums. Several of these possible suspects were Jews.

Caged in an Asylum

Sir Robert Anderson, assistant commissioner of police, was the official most firmly convinced that the Ripper was mad. Describing the investigation, Anderson later wrote in a magazine piece:

> One does not have to be a Sherlock Holmes to discover that the criminal was a . . . maniac of a virulent type; that he was living in the immediate vicinity of the scenes of the murders; and that, if he was not living absolutely alone, his people knew of his guilt, and refused to give him up to justice. . . . The police had made a house-to-house search for him, investigating . . . every man in the district whose circumstances were such that he could go and come and get rid of his blood-stains in secret. And the conclusion we came to was that he and his people were low-class Jews. [48]

Anderson's belief was shared, to some extent, by Melville McNaughten. A memorandum written by McNaughten confirms that a Jewish man named Aaron Kosminski was a serious suspect during the hunt for Jack the Ripper. McNaughten wrote:

No one ever saw the Whitechapel murderer, many homicidal maniacs were suspected, but no shadow of proof could be thrown on any one. I may mention the cases of 3 men, any one of whom would have been . . . likely . . . to have committed this series of murders. . . . [One was] Kosminski, a Polish Jew, & resident in Whitechapel. This man became insane. . . . He had a great hatred of women, specially of the prostitute class, & had strong homicidal tendencies; he was removed to a lunatic asylum about March 1889 & had strong suicidal tendencies. There were many circs [circumstances] connected with this man which made him a strong "suspect."[49]

Yet in naming this suspect, McNaughten only added to the mystery of Jack the Ripper's identity.

Historians have been unable to locate any asylum records for Kosminski, either in or near London, in 1889. Only in 1891 does the name "Kosminski" appear. The inmate it describes, though, was not violent. Did McNaughten, when writing his piece, make a mistake? Ripper enthusiast Martin Fido thinks that McNaughten may have misremembered another name—that of Nathan Kaminsky, a Jewish man who was placed in an asylum shortly after the autumn of terror. Yet Fido argues that it is even more likely that still another working-class Jewish man, incarcerated for mad behavior, might have been the suicidal lunatic referred to by McNaughten.

David Cohen—referred to in some asylum records as Aaron Davis Cohen—was destructive, a danger to himself and others in the asylum. He was, in Fido's words, "far and away the most violent lunatic to enter the asylum in . . . [that] period."[50] The brutal murders most often attributed to Jack the Ripper ceased when Cohen was removed from the streets of Whitechapel in 1889. But how could McNaughten and others have confused "Cohen" with "Kosminski"? Fido and other historians point out that Cohen's real name might well have been Kosminski. British officials, having little patience or appreciation for the foreign names of eastern European Jews, frequently listed all Jews in routine paperwork as "Cohen." In this limited sense, prejudice against foreigners and Jews might have contributed to the many mysteries surrounding Jack the Ripper.

Some Londoners believed the killer was Jewish. Here, a policeman examines graffiti near the Catherine Eddowes crime scene, which reads: "The Jews are the men that will not be blamed for nothing."

"The Greatest . . . of All Russian Lunatics"

McNaughten also named another immigrant, a Russian barber whose earlier training as a surgeon's assistant might explain the Ripper's terrible proficiency with a knife. According to McNaughten, this man was "Michael Ostrog, a Russian doctor, and a convict, who was subsequently detained in a lunatic asylum as a [suspected] homicidal maniac. The man's [past deeds] were of the worst possible type, and his whereabouts at the time of the murders could never be ascertained."[51] Ostrog, though, had a long history as a thief rather than as a person who committed violent crimes. During the autumn of terror, he was not hunted by police in the way Aaron Kosminski and other men were. Yet Ostrog's identification by McNaughten did bring to light another suspect in the search for Jack the Ripper.

According to some historians, police officers hunting the Ripper discovered a strong physical resemblance between the dark-haired, bearded Ostrog and another Russian immigrant. This man, Alexander Pedachenko, had also been a surgeon's assistant. Pedachenko had episodes of violent insanity. He had even been convicted and imprisoned for brutal knife attacks against women in his Russian hometown. Was it really Pedachenko that police should have taken in for questioning?

Also, what had led the violent Pedachenko to the dark streets of Whitechapel? Perhaps there was a sinister reason behind his presence there. Historians later discovered a report in a Russian police journal that told a strange tale about this madman: that Pedachenko was not only Jack the Ripper, but that he acted with the support of Russian authorities. It claimed that Russian secret police

> had themselves actively encouraged and aided the [Ripper's] crimes, in order to exhibit to the world certain defects of the English police system. It was . . . for that reason that Pedachenko, the greatest and boldest of all Russian lunatics, was encouraged to go to

London to commit the series of atrocious crimes, in which aspects of [the Russian] police aided him.

Such are the actual facts of the Jack the Ripper mystery which still puzzles the world.[52]

If this report is true, cold and deliberate calculation on the part of others was behind the acts of the Whitechapel Murderer. Its truth, however, like much surrounding this case, remains in doubt. It is possible that a Russian, fascinated by these unsolved crimes or boastful about Russian ingenuity, made up this tale.

While Ostrog and Pedachenko were two of the early suspects in these crimes, most people today do not place either of them among those still suspected of being the Ripper. However, some still do believe they had a connection to the case.

"The Best Thing for Me Was to Die"
The third suspect McNaughten named, Montague John Druitt, was the only one who matched the superficially sane, "gentleman" killer described by Winslow. According to McNaughten, Jack the Ripper could well have been

> a Mr. M.J. Druitt, said to be a doctor & of good family, who disapppeared at the time of the Miller's Court [Kelly's] murder, & whose body (which was said to have been upwards of a month in the water) was found in the Thames [River] on 31st [December], about 7 weeks after that murder. He was . . . insane.[53]

M.J. Druitt was thirty-one years old at the time of his death, an age that matched many witness accounts of possible Ripper sightings. His dress—genteel rather than rough, workingman's clothes—also matched some eyewitness descriptions of the Ripper. Perhaps of greatest significance to McNaughten, though, was the fact that Druitt was mentally disturbed. McNaughten felt that Druitt's suicide supported

his conviction that Jack the Ripper (Druitt) was mentally ill. But what evidence did the police have against Druitt?

Records show that Druitt was upset because his mother, a longtime sufferer of mental illness, had been locked away in an asylum just four months earlier. Others in his family had also been afflicted with mental problems. Druitt left his brother a note, explaining, "Since Friday I felt I was going to be like mother, and the best thing for me was to die."[54] Druitt then, it seemed, placed four large stones in each of his coat pockets and waded to his death in the murky Thames. Beyond these apparent facts, though, and their occurrence so soon after Mary Jane Kelly's murder, there seems little to connect Druitt to the Whitechapel murders.

Druitt did not live in or have detailed knowledge of this grim area, with its dark, narrow streets. He did not have a history of being violent. Druitt did not even have the surgical skills of a doctor. McNaughten misremembered or misunderstood this suspect's background. It was Druitt's father who had been a doctor, while M.J. Druitt himself was a lawyer and part-time schoolteacher. Also, Druitt was thin and athletic, not a match for the several eyewitness reports that described the Ripper as a heavyset man. It is not surprising, then, that some police disagreed about Druitt's having been Jack the Ripper. As Inspector Abberline, actively involved in the case, remarked in a 1903 newspaper interview:

> Soon after the last murder in Whitechapel the body of a young doctor was found in the Thames, but there is nothing beyond the fact that he was found at that time to incriminate him. A report was made to the Home Office about [Druitt's being the Ripper], but that it was "considered final and conclusive" is going altogether beyond the truth. Seeing the same kind of murders began in America afterwards, there is much more reason to think [Jack the Ripper] emigrated. Then, again, the fact that several months after December, 1888, when [Druitt's] ... body was found, the detectives were told to hold themselves in readiness for further investigations seems to point to the conclusion that Scotland Yard did not in any way consider the evidence as final. [55]

While some police officials told members of vigilance committees that there was no further threat from the Ripper, that this killer had drowned in the Thames when Druitt did, others disagreed. Except for Robert Anderson, most police believed that if Jack was indeed a maniac, he was most likely a working-class one, unlike the genteel Druitt.

If M.J. Druitt was not himself the Ripper, did this unhappy person play another role in this series of crimes? Perhaps Druitt's drowning was not suicide but actually murder, committed to protect the real identity of the Whitechapel Murderer. By providing officials with a likely suspect who could not protest his guilt, Druitt's death might have directed investigators away

Inspector Abberline, played here by Michael Caine (kneeling) in a television movie, discounted M.J. Druitt as a Ripper suspect.

A modern Ripper theory suggests the killer murdered the women to prevent them from exposing Prince Albert Victor Edward's (pictured) marriage to a working-class woman.

from other suspects or even closed the case. This idea is part of one complicated theory about Jack the Ripper. In this view of the Ripper's identity and motives, the Whitechapel slayings were not the acts of a madman. Instead, they were acts of carefully calculated and savage sanity.

"Not One Man but Three"

According to this theory, the Whitechapel murders were cold-bloodedly committed to protect the reputation of a member of the British royal family, Prince Albert Victor Edward. This grandson of Queen Victoria, known informally as "Eddie," was twenty-four years old during the autumn of terror. According to Ripper historian Stephen Knight, Eddie had secretly married a young woman of whom his family never approved. Annie

Crook was both Roman Catholic and working-class, and her acquaintances included prostitutes such as Mary Kelly. It was a marriage the royal family refused to accept. Perhaps by direct orders, or possibly through indirect hints, they set in motion events that led to the Ripper slayings.

Knight and some others believe that the royal physician, Dr. William Gull, tried to remove all evidence of this marriage. Gull, they say, had Annie Crook wrongfully placed in a mental asylum. He then unsuccessfully ordered the death of Annie and Eddie's toddler daughter. Knight also maintains that Mary Kelly knew about these misdeeds, and that Kelly—together with her friends Mary Ann Nichols, Annie Chapman, Elizabeth Stride, and Catherine Eddowes—later foolishly tried to blackmail the royal family with this information. They had to be silenced. The Whitechapel slayings, then, were not random acts committed by a madman, but the deliberate execution of women who had threatened to reveal scandalous royal secrets. As Knight writes about these East End murders: "Jack the Ripper is a misnomer. The name conjures up visions of a lone assassin. . . . This mistaken notion, inspired by that terrifying nickname . . . rendered the murder of five East End prostitutes insoluble. For Jack the Ripper was not one man but three, two killers and an accomplice." [56]

In Knight's theory of this case, the main killer was Gull himself, while the accomplice was his coach driver, William Netley. Perhaps Netley, under orders from Gull, murdered M.J. Druitt to provide police with the "maniac" they believed they were hunting. The second killer was most likely Walter Sickert, a young artist whose studio was in the East End.

A number of people disagree with this idea of a royal conspiracy being the cause of the Ripper's carnage. They point to Gull's age and health; Gull was seventy years old in 1888, and he had suffered a mild stroke a few years earlier. They doubt that he had the strength to commit the Ripper's brutal deeds. People who agree with Knight emphasize other points. They note that Gull was reported as being active even after his stroke. They argue that Dr. Gull had the surgical skills that several coroners said were evident in the Ripper's mutilations. They maintain that Gull was able to slay Catherine Eddowes less than an hour after attacking Elizabeth Stride because he was driven swiftly between the crime sites in Netley's coach.

In this conspiracy theory of the case, one small, mysterious detail also takes on surprising importance. Witness

Some believe that the royal physician William Gull committed the Ripper crimes with the help of two accomplices.

Matthew Packard claimed to have sold grapes to Elizabeth Stride and an unknown man shortly before her death. A police officer thought he saw grape seeds and stems near her body. These reports may be evidence that Gull was at the crime scene. In a letter written to a medical colleague, Gull describes a habit for which he was well-known:

> When fatigued I personally refreshed myself by eating raisins. I have been in the habit of doing this for many years. I never travel or may I say go anwhere without raisins. They are always in my travelling bag. . . . I eat no cane sugar but the sugar of the grape seems to supply the readiest refreshing material of which I have in my own person any experience. . . . when fatigued I prefer grapes and raisins and water. [57]

Stephen Knight believes that the grape seeds and stems possibly seen on that dirty Whitechapel street near Elizabeth Stride's corpse were telltale clues left by Gull. Yet many people disagree. They note that garbage often littered those grimy alleys. People also disagree with Knight's explanation of why Gull mutilated the victims.

"Heart and Vitals Taken"

According to Knight, Gull was a longtime member of a fraternal organization called the Freemasons. Begun centuries ago by men, such as masons, who worked with stone or brick in the building trades, this group admits members who swear to support and help one another. Its members have traditions and rituals that they keep secret from outsiders. The secrecy of these rituals has sometimes made non-Masons very suspicious of this group.

Knight argues that the Ripper's mutilations reproduce the horrible death one famous traitor to the Masons had wished upon himself. This traitor, Jebelow, supposedly said, "O that my left breast had been torn open and my heart and vitals taken from thence and thrown over my left shoulder." [58] Knight

believes that Gull mutilated the would-be blackmailers of the royal family because they, too, were traitors. This mutilation was also Gull's bizarre way of showing his ongoing loyalty to and belief in Freemasonry.

Perhaps such loyalty even determined Gull's choice of a second killer to assist him with these slayings. Knight names Walter Sickert, a successful painter, as this second killer, but other people maintain that Gull involved a fellow Mason, Assistant Police Commissioner Sir Robert Anderson himself, in these crimes. They name Anderson as the second killer

Dr. William Gull belonged to the fraternal Freemasons organization, whose gathering hall in London is pictured here.

involved in this conspiracy. They also say that the many changes in senior-level police staff during the Ripper case were arranged by Masons to help Gull.

Historian Philip Sugden, however, points out that the Ripper's mutilations do not really follow Mason Jebelow's terrible instructions. Sugden writes:

> In the cases of both Chapman and Eddowes, the intestines, not the heart and chest contents, were lifted out, and they were placed over the right, not the left shoulders. . . . [Mary Kelly's] viscera and detached flesh were left in various places—under her hand, by her right foot, between her feet, by her right or left side, and heaped upon a bedside table, in short almost everywhere *except* over her left shoulder.[59]

Sugden concludes that only by omitting or distorting evidence could anyone argue that the Ripper's victims displayed a pattern of mutilations supporting this Masonic conspiracy theory. Yet this far-fetched theory of Jack the Ripper's identity and motives is among the best known today. It has even been used for the plot of four films made about this mysterious series of crimes. Depicting this serial killer as a cruelly rational man who skillfully employs others as he executes his careful plans, these films keep alive the disturbing, still unanswered question: Was Jack the Ripper mad . . . or sane?

Chapter 4

Was His Motive Hatred or Love?

S trong emotions such as anger or jealousy often fuel crimes of violence. What feelings, though, might have motivated the prolonged butchery of Jack the Ripper? This mystery has never been solved. Some people believe the Ripper probably killed out of deep-seated hatred; others maintain that this murderer, using his own twisted logic, actually killed out of love.

"Such Masses of Evil"

Some people, known as misogynists, irrationally despise all women. The hatred of women expressed by poet James Stephen briefly made him a suspect in this case. Stephen wrote:

> If all the harm that women have done,
> Were put in a bottle and rolled into one,
> Earth would not hold it,
> The sky could not enfold it,
> It could not be lighted nor warmed by the sun;
>
> Such masses of evil
> Would puzzle the devil,
> And keep him in fuel while Time's wheels run. [60]

Believing women evil enough to perplex the devil, Stephen might have been convinced that the Whitechapel slayings were justified. This twenty-nine-year-old poet and journalist was also known to have a short temper, made worse by a head injury he had suffered in 1886. It left Stephen irritable enough to wish a man dead merely for stepping on his foot in a crowded train. This brain injury ultimately led to Stephen's early death, at the age of thirty-three, in 1892.

Beyond Stephen's intense hatred of women, though, there is little to connect this misogynist to the Whitechapel slayings. It was only Stephen's social involvement with other individuals tied to the case that brought him to police attention. The poet was acquainted with Prince Eddie and was said to have known M.J. Druitt. These associations led to

In the 1978 film Murder by Decree, *the fictional detectives Sherlock Holmes (right) and Dr. Watson consider all suspects in the Ripper case.*

Stephen's being mentioned in a few police documents and unofficial records kept about the Ripper's crimes. Later, these notes captured the attention of some Ripper hunters. Yet this well-born poet was not familiar with the narrow streets of London's East End, and he did not resemble any of the eyewitness descriptions of possible Ripper sightings. Stephen also had no history of physically attacking women.

Misogynist poet James Stephen was dismissed as a suspect because he was unfamiliar with the Whitechapel District. Pictured is the street where Mary Ann Nichols was found.

Today, most people agree that James Stephen is one of the least likely candidates of all those proposed as the Whitechapel killer. Yet this poet's expression of misogyny gives voice to the emotions of a much less articulate woman hater whom many people do consider a likely suspect in these brutal slayings.

"A Sharp and Formidable Knife"

Severin Klosowski (later also known as George Chapman) immigrated to London shortly before the Ripper killings began, most likely in March 1887. In his native Poland, Klosowski had spent five years as an assistant surgeon. He had the medical skills many coroners believed were so gruesomely displayed by the Ripper. Once in England, Klosowski worked in or owned a series of barber shops in Whitechapel. He was well acquainted with the area and would not have had to travel far either to find his victims or to wash up after mutilating them.

Much more than background and location, though, suggest that Severin Klosowski may have been Jack the Ripper. He had a history of disdain and violence toward women. As one of his wives, Lucy Klosowski, later told a newspaper reporter:

> On one occasion [when they quarrelled] . . . her husband . . . held her down on the bed, and pressed his face against her mouth to keep her from screaming. At that moment a customer entered the shop immediately in front of the room, and Klosowski got up to attend him. [Lucy] chanced to see a handle protruding from underneath the pillow. She found, to her horror, that it was a sharp and formidable knife, which she promptly hid. Later, Klosowski deliberately told her that he meant to have cut her head off, and pointed to a place in the room where he meant to have buried her. She said, "But the neighbors would have

asked where I had gone to." "Oh," retorted Klosowski calmly, "I should simply have told them that you had gone [away]."[61]

Klosowski's subsequent actions suggest that this was not an empty threat. In the decade following the Whitechapel killings, he poisoned to death three women with whom he lived, including one whose last name, Chapman, he unofficially adopted as his own. He left a clear trail of purchasing the kind of slow-acting, painful poison discovered in the body of each victim. Calling himself "George Chapman," this serial murderer was also known to have brutally beaten at least four other women. When George Chapman was arrested and tried for the murder of poisoned Maud Marsh, it took a jury only eleven minutes to find him guilty. On April 7, 1903, without ever expressing any remorse for his crimes, George Chapman was executed in Britain's Wadsworth Prison.

Inspector Abberline, who was active in the hunt for the Ripper, reportedly said to the police officer who had arrested Chapman, "You've got the Ripper at last!"[62] Abberline had noted that the murders most often attributed to the mysterious Whitechapel killer not only began when Chapman arrived in London but also stopped when he briefly immigrated to the United States. During this period between April 1891 and June 1892, when Chapman was in New York and New Jersey, at least one Ripper-like slaying—and possibly two others—also took place in those states. Abberline believed that these events were more than coincidence; they were circumstantial evidence that pointed directly to Severin Klosowski, also known as George Chapman.

"His Diabolical Cunning"

Yet not everyone was firmly convinced that the Ripper had indeed been caught. Twenty-three at the time of the Whitechapel murders, Chapman was younger than eyewitness reports of a possible killer in his late twenties or early thirties. Chapman also dressed in shabby clothes, unlike the neat and better quality garments described by some eyewitnesses. Chapman was clean shaven, while many witnesses claimed to have seen the Ripper's victims talking to a man with a mustache. Finally, Severin Klosowski spoke sometimes ungrammatical English with a Polish accent; his speech was unlike that of the refined, unaccented words supposedly overheard by several eyewitnesses.

Some of these doubts are quickly brushed aside today by Ripper historian Michael Gordon, who believes George Chapman was indeed the Ripper. Gordon claims that photographs show Chapman looked older than his years, that even shabbily dressed people may own fancier clothing, and that a false mustache may be used as a disguise. Gordon also dismisses a point that troubled trained investigators then and now: Would a serial murderer change his method of killing?

According to modern criminologist John Douglas, George Chapman could not have been the Ripper because "there is no way a man hacks apart five or six women, lies low for ten years with no one noticing anything about him, then resumes his homicidal career as a poisoner. . . . It just doesn't happen that way in real life."[63]

Yet police superintendent Arthur Neil believed this was what happened. Writing in the 1930s about the Ripper, Neil said Chapman switched methods to avoid detection. He "took to poisoning his victims on his second visit to [Britain because of] his diabolical cunning."[64] Inspector Abberline also dismissed questions about this dramatic change in murderous techniques. Abberline responded:

> As to the dissimilarity of the character of the crimes . . . I cannot see why one man should not have done both, provided he had the professional knowledge, and this is admitted in Chapman's case. A man who could watch his wives being slowly tortured to death by poison, as he did, was capable of anything, and the

Rumor and Speculation

Who Was Jack the Ripper?

The Ripper might have been:

In his late 20s to early 30s • Well-dressed • Of medium height • Heavyset •
Wearing a moustache • A madman • A women-hater • Surgically skilled •
Using a knife like those of doctors or butchers

A Sampling of Suspects

Joseph Barnett, 30
Roomed with victim Mary Jane Kelley • Job was cleaning and gutting fish •
Proficient with knives

David Cohen, 23
Violent • Jewish Whitechapel resident • Insane asylum inmate

Montague John Druitt, 31
Thin and athletic • Mentally disturbed • Genteel dress and family background •
No surgical skills

Dr. William Gull, 70
Physician to England's royal family • Suspected of having two accomplices in
the murders

George Hutchinson, age unknown
Fit a witness description of the Ripper • Knew Mary Jane Kelly • Claimed he
saw the Ripper with Kelly

Severin Klosowski (also known as George Chapman), 23
Shabbily dressed • Clean-shaven • Assistant surgeon and barber • Whitechapel
resident • Violent toward women • In United States at time of several Ripper-
like murders there • Killed other women after the Ripper killings had ended

Aaron Kosminski, 23–24
Madman • Jewish • Hated prostitutes • Lived in Whitechapel

James Maybrick, 50
A diary purported to be his contained confession that he was the Ripper

Alexander Pedachenko, 30-ish
Surgeon's assistant • Insane and violent • Russian • Imprisoned for brutally
knifing women in Russia

Walter Sickert, 28
Artist • Prostitutes posed for him • Painted chilling scenes of facially-mutilated
women • Fascinated with crime and criminals • May have been murder accomplice of Dr. Gull

Francis Tumblety, 55
Taller and older than Ripper descriptions • A "quack" doctor • Anger toward
women • American • Collected anatomical specimens • American newspapers
reported him as a suspect

fact that he should have attempted . . . to murder his first wife with a knife in NJ, makes one inclined to believe . . . he was mixed up in the two series of crimes. [65]

If George Chapman was Jack the Ripper, he changed his brutal method of slaughter in a way that still mystifies some people. Yet Chapman was not the only savage person walking the streets of Whitechapel in 1888 who was filled with hatred towards women.

"Into Such Danger"

Francis Tumblety had a criminal past and great anger toward women. The son of Irish immigrants to the United States, Tumblety had grown up in Rochester, New York. There, he worked for a doctor, sold fake patent medicines, and—pretending to be a doctor himself—illegally began to practice medicine. This practice included providing abortions for prostitutes. Tumblety was arrested when one of his patients died after taking the so-called medicine Tumblety had prescribed. This quack doctor then fled the state to avoid trial.

Tumblety spent time in Canada as well as Great Britain. He continued to trick money out of people, dressing extravagantly and often inviting well-to-do potential customers to dinner. Women were not welcome at these gatherings. When asked why he would not invite women, one guest recalled that Tumblety replied

> almost savagely . . . [with a] face instantly as black as a thundercloud. He said . . . "I don't know any such cattle, and if I did I would, as your friend, sooner give you a dose of quick poison than take you into such danger." He then . . . fiercely denounced all women and especially fallen women.

> He illustrated the lecture. . . . One side of [his office] was occupied with cases. . . . When the doors were opened . . . [there were] shelves with glass jars . . . filled

with all sorts of anatomical specimens . . . the [uteri] of every class of women. . . .

When asked why he hated women, [Tumblety] said when quite a young man he fell desperately in love . . . he married her. . . . Happening one day to pass in a cab through the worst part of town he saw his wife and a man enter a gloomy looking house. Then he learned that before his marriage his wife had [been a prostitute] in that and many similar houses. Then he gave up on mankind.[66]

While Tumblety's explanation of his feelings may have been as false as his claim to be a doctor, his hatred of women was real. This misogynist, who had some medical knowledge and kept a gruesome collection of body parts, lived in London during the autumn of terror. He may even have rented a room in the East End, close to the Whitechapel crime scenes. It seems that Francis Tumblety had the motive, means, and access needed to commit the Whitechapel murders.

Travel records show that Tumblety boarded a ship for the United States on November 24, 1888. He never returned to Great Britain. If Mary Jane Kelly was truly the Ripper's last London victim, killed on November 9, then Tumblety was present in London for all five murders generally ascribed to the brutal Whitechapel killer. Tumblety's departure would also explain why the slaughter stopped then. If, however, as some people believe, there were later victims, Tumblety could not have committed those later crimes, and the hunt for the Ripper must move on to other suspects.

Even if the quack doctor remains a suspect, other mysteries still surround Francis Tumblety. These include when and by whom he was seriously suspected of being the Ripper.

"Bitter in the Extreme"

For more than a hundred years, Francis Tumblety's possible involvement in this notorious criminal case was almost unknown. Even many dedicated Ripperologists had not heard of him. Then, in 1993, Ripper historian Stewart Evans was contacted by an antique book seller. This man had just acquired an old letter mentioning Jack the Ripper that he believed would interest Evans. In fact, Evans and several oth-

Researchers continue to probe the mysteries of the Ripper case. The Whitechapel District of the Ripper era is today an upscale neighborhood.

er Ripper historians were amazed by this letter, written in September 1913 by former chief inspector John Littlechild. In it, Littlechild seems to be responding to a well-known journalist's question about a Ripper suspect called "Dr. D." Littlechild replies:

> I never heard of a Dr. D. in connection with the Whitechapel murders but amongst the suspects, and to my mind a very likely one, was a Dr. T. (which sounds much like D). He was an American quack named Tumblety and was at one time a frequent visitor to London and on these occasions constantly brought under the notice of police, there being a large dossier [file] concerning him at Scotland Yard. . . . His feelings towards women were remarkable and bitter in the extreme, a fact on record. [67]

After having historians and scientists verify that this letter was genuine, Evans and others set out to discover more about the mysterious Dr. T. They learned that Francis Tumblety's homosexual activities, then illegal in Great Britain, had led to the large file about him at Scotland Yard. It is unclear whether Tumblety was ever suspected by British police of being the Ripper. Other suspects, however slight or even absurd the charges against them, are mentioned as such in police documents and unofficial communications from that period. Tumblety is not. The British press, so eager for news about the Ripper that it printed even wild claims, never mentioned Tumblety in this context. Yet this quack doctor, upon his return to the United States in the late autumn of 1888, was reported as a Ripper suspect by several American newspapers. An article in the December 4, 1888, issue of the *Trenton (New Jersey) Times* noted: "Francis Tumblety . . . , who was arrested in London for supposed complicity in Whitechapel Crimes and held under bail for other offenses, arrived in [New York City] Sunday, and is now stopping in East Tenth Street. Two of

Inspector Byrnes' men are watching him and so is an English detective."[68]

Newspapers in New York, Washington, D.C., Kansas, California, Georgia, and even Canada also mentioned Tumblety as a Ripper suspect. Yet New York City inspector Byrnes, while "keep[ing Tumblety] in view as a matter of ordinary precaution . . . laugh[ed] at the suggestion that [Tumblety] was the Whitechapel murderer."[69]

Likewise, it is possible that British police never considered Tumblety a serious suspect. Some historians note that the British detective watching Tumblety in New York was originally sent across the Atlantic on another case. This detective was only available by chance. These historians also note that Tumblety was taller, older, and had a much fuller mustache than the man described by Ripper eyewitnesses. There is a possibility, too, that Tumblety—under arrest in Britain in early November 1888 for homosexual acts—might not have been released in time to murder Mary Jane Kelly on November 9. For these reasons, some historians dismiss the importance of Littlechild's letter and the North American newspaper articles that sensationalized Tumblety's return from Britain. They doubt that Tumblety could have been the Ripper or that he was ever under active, serious investigation.

If hatred of women did not motivate the Whitechapel Murderer's gruesome crimes, could they have been inspired in some perverted way by love? This horrifying possibility has also been explored in the search for Jack the Ripper.

"My Knifes So Nice and Sharp"

According to historian Bruce Paley, it was desperate love for one woman that motivated the Ripper's butchery. Paley believes that Joseph Barnett, who had shared lodgings with Mary Jane Kelly, was the Whitechapel killer. This historian claims that the jealous Barnett killed his first victims to frighten Kelly away from prostitution. When this attempt

failed, Paley says that Barnett slaughtered Kelly in one last, frustrated, murderous rage. Barnett was obsessed with this woman. Paley notes that Kelly's youth and beauty, rare in dismal Whitechapel, drew Barnett to her as honey draws flies. While Barnett still held his well-paying job as a laborer in London's fish market, Kelly did not need to prostitute herself. Several months before the Ripper killings began, though, Barnett lost this job. To Barnett's dismay, Kelly returned to prostitution. Neighbors and acquaintances remembered

A knife like the one the Ripper may have used is shown here with a drawing of one of his victims. Since he gutted fish for a living, Joseph Barnett's cutting skills may have equaled the Ripper's.

violent quarrels between the couple, ending in Barnett's moving out of their shared room.

Barnett's lost job may be further evidence of the jealous man's inclination toward violence and his ability to brutally dissect the Whitechapel victims. For more than a decade, he had carried, cleaned, and gutted fish. As Paley observes: "Research . . . has revealed that serial killers have been known to take jobs in which they can vicariously experience their morbid, destructive fantasies. For Joseph Barnett, it was no great leap from gutting fish to mutilating women."[70] This observation, in a more general way, was even made during the autumn of terror. As coroners speculated about the Ripper's possible medical training, one physician who had spent time at sea noted that "the great surgical skill which [Jack the Ripper] used to apply to his female victims could easily have been picked up by a man accustomed to boning and filleting fish."[71]

Some historians note that Barnett was in the habit of reading a daily newspaper to the illiterate Kelly. He would have seen how frightened this young woman was by reports of earlier brutal crimes in the East End. Her reactions might have inspired Barnett—maddened by jealous love—to commit the series of bloody murders that began with the slaughter of Mary Ann Nichols. Paley believes that Barnett wrote the bloodthirsty letters sent by Jack the Ripper, filling them with gory details and threats, just to terrify Kelly with them once they appeared in print. Threats such as "My knifes so nice and sharp I want to get to work right away if I get a chance,"[72] read aloud by Barnett in bloodcurdling tones, were supposed to scare Kelly off Whitechapel's dark streets. According to Paley, it was the failure of this plan that led to Barnett's final act of madness—the murder and grotesque mutilation of the woman who refused to be his alone.

Joseph Barnett was familiar with Whitechapel's streets and alleys; he would have known shortcuts that gave the Ripper easy, quick access to victims. Paley also believes that the site of Mary Jane Kelly's death is significant. Who else besides Joseph Barnett would have had access to that locked room? Who else besides a maddened lover would have carried away the heart of the woman he had just killed? Yet there are answers to these questions that only add to the mysteries surrounding this case. A broken window might have permitted the Ripper to enter the locked room. Coroners' reports are unclear about whether Kelly's heart was actually removed from the blood-drenched room or just placed alongside her. There is no conclusive evidence that proves Joseph Barnett was Jack the Ripper.

"Mission from Above"

There are even theories that suggest a different kind of love might have motivated this serial killer. During the autumn of terror, some people wondered whether a distorted love of God might be behind the crimes. A letter published in the London *Times* asked if Jack the Ripper might be

> an earnest religionist with a delusion that he has a mission from above to extirpate [end] vice by assassination. And he has selected his victims from a class which contributes pretty largely to . . . immorality and sin. I have known men and women actuated [impelled] by the best and purest motives who have been dominated by an insane passion of this kind, and who honestly believed that by its indulgence they would be doing good service.[73]

Perhaps, another person suggested, the Ripper was actually two or more people—devout Christian missionaries working together. Such a pair had recently been seen in the East End. Two killers, each attacking a different victim, might explain how Catherine Eddowes had been murdered within an hour of Elizabeth Stride. These men might have shared a twisted idea of religious love that caused them to kill and mutilate Whitechapel prostitutes. This theory appeared in another letter to a London newspaper. Its author believed that the Whitechapel murders were committed "with the view of terrifying the women of the district into abandoning their way of life."[74] This possibility was among the many unlikely ideas followed up by desperate police during the autumn of terror. As others did, it seemed to lead nowhere.

Hatred or love? Investigations of the Whitechapel murders reveal several suspects who each displayed strong emotion. To this day, though, which emotion might have motivated Jack the Ripper remains a mystery.

Chapter 5

Does Science Have the Answer?

I n the last quarter century, scientific advances have been made in investigating crime. Will these new techniques help solve this mysterious case? Some historians speculated that the answers might be found through old-fashioned detective work, once all the evidence was available.

In 1988, one hundred years after the autumn of terror, sealed police records about the Ripper were made public. Perhaps these documents would yield new clues to the brutal killer's identity. Excited Ripperologists eagerly pored over the three, brown-wrapped bundles of paper. Yet their inspection revealed little not already known.

"Hoping for Startling Revelations"
Two of the files were overflowing with the letters that disturbed individuals, along with concerned citizens, had sent about the Ripper. The third file was filled with official reports, many handwritten at the actual crime scenes. Often, this faded handwriting was difficult to read and identify. Some reports were incomplete or missing. A few Ripperologists wondered if a conspiracy lay behind these missing records.

Historian Donald Rumbelow, a former London detective, has a more likely explanation for the missing documents. Rumbelow observes that many police records over the years were lost or destroyed through accident or neglect. Sometimes, he ruefully notes, "It was quite customary when more space was needed for the [workers] to yank out handfuls of papers from old files to make way for new ones. . . . Anyone who is hoping for startling revelations from the Jack the Ripper file will be very disappointed."[75]

Ripperologists abandoned the hope that official records had, for whatever reason, contained well-guarded secrets about the Whitechapel murders. They turned, instead, to science to reexamine items linked to past suspects in these serial killings. Recently, science has also been used to investigate a new suspect who has appeared in the ongoing hunt for the Ripper's true identity.

"My Fiendish Deeds"

Perhaps James Maybrick, an English cotton merchant who died in 1889, was really Jack the Ripper. In 1991, Maybrick's supposed diary was discovered. In it, Maybrick details an account of the Whitechapel murders and confesses to being the Ripper. He writes of being jealous both of his wife, whom he suspects of infidelity, and of another woman in Whitechapel he also loves. In the diary's first entry, Maybrick scribbles, "They will suffer just as I."[76] Later, the unhappy man notes, "My hands are cold, my heart I do believe is colder still."[77] After describing several murders in gruesome detail, Maybrick adds, "When I have finished my fiendish deeds, the devil himself will praise me."[78] Maybrick concludes his confession with these emotional words: "I give my name that all know of me, so history do tell, what love can do to a gentle man born. Yours truly, Jack the Ripper. Dated this day of May 1889."[79]

Eight days later, James Maybrick died, addicted to arsenic, a dangerous chemical then used in some medicines. His fatal symptoms were those of arsenic poisoning. It is unclear, however, if the addicted Maybrick unknowingly poisoned himself or if his wife, Florrie, deliberately poisoned him. His death was suspicious enough that Mrs. Maybrick was arrested, tried, and convicted for her husband's murder. Fifteen years passed before her life sentence was overturned.

Cotton merchant James Maybrick's diary, in which he confessed that he was the Ripper, was found shortly before he died. However, the diary's authenticity is questionable.

Florrie Maybrick appears in court during her trial for the murder of her husband. Fifteen years after the trial, her conviction was overturned.

The sensational trial of Florrie Maybrick for her husband's death made them well-known figures in Victorian England. Newspaper accounts of the couple's lives helped Ripperologists who sought to verify the facts of the diary, which was written in the pages of a photograph album. They could use these reports and trial records to see how well James Maybrick's comings and goings matched events in the Whitechapel murders. Yet there was an even more basic question that had to be asked about the diary: Was it authentic, or a modern fraud?

This question became more urgent in 1993 as its purported discoverers tried to have it published. Concerned publishers and Ripperologists turned to science for the answers.

To their dismay, scientific testing to determine the age of the diary's ink and paper was inconclusive. One test suggested the ink was a kind still in use today; others dated the ink back to 1920, possibly as far back as 1900. Could that time range legitimately be extended even further backward to 1888? Scientific examination of the paper in the Maybrick diary proved that *it* was authentic, manufactured in or before the autumn of terror. Yet the authenticity of the diary overall remained debatable. Document analysts, trained to examine handwriting, only added to this mystery when they noted that the diary's handwriting did not match the signature on James Maybrick's will. They also said that a real diary, written in many times throughout a year, would not have the even ink use and handwriting displayed in the Maybrick diary.

Then, in 1993, a watch purportedly belonging to James Maybrick was discovered. Scratched into its metal surface were the words "J. Maybrick," "I am Jack," and the initials of the Ripper's five best-known victims. Here was new evidence that could be tested scientifically. Using an electron microscope, metallurgists proved that the scratches were at least one hundred years old. The watch could indeed have been carried by Jack the Ripper as he committed his bloody crimes. Yet skeptics maintained that the age of the watch and paper did not prove that their words were true.

"Jack the Ripoff?"

Perhaps a contemporary of the Maybricks, reading about Florrie's sensational trial, had forged the diary and enhanced this lie with the scratchings on the back of the watch. Skeptics pointed out that it was unlikely that James Maybrick, a well-to-do merchant, would have reused a torn photograph album for his diary. They also noted that the watch was one usually worn by women. In July 1993, the *Washington Post* featured an article about James Maybrick subtitled "Jack the Ripoff?" that condemned the Maybrick confession as a fraud. This article publicized objections skeptics had raised about Maybrick as a possible suspect in the Whitechapel murders.

Publicity from the trial of Florrie Maybrick (pictured) may have led someone to forge the diary in which James Maybrick admitted to being the Ripper.

A few months later, an article in the London *Sunday Times* explained how greed might have motivated this fraud. The newspaper's publisher had been asked to buy the Maybrick story. Its seller even insisted that the *Times* keep this purchase a secret. The *Times* reporter wrote:

> Robert Smith approached the Sunday *Times* . . . early . . . this year and claimed he had a "sensational document." At subsequent meetings he revealed he had acquired the rights to the Ripper diary and knew exactly who he was: James Maybrick. The Sunday *Times* was required to pay a non-returnable 5,000 pounds [about 10,000 dollars today] for an option to take up the serial rights, and to sign a series of confidentiality agreements. [80]

Even if the Maybrick diary was a hoax begun in the 1890s, people a century later were eager to make a profit from this document. The *Times* went on to "warn the public that there was a danger of the Ripper's forged confessions . . . becom[ing] the biggest international fraud in the book world." [81]

Today, the mystery of James Maybrick's supposed confession remains unsolved. Science has, to date, provided conflicting answers about the document's age. While some Ripperologists believe that Maybrick may have been the Ripper, many others disagree. They point to discrepancies between Maybrick's account of the Whitechapel murders and police records of the crimes. In this case, old-fashioned detective work may ultimately be more conclusive than current scientific tests.

"What Might Be Blood"

Science is also being used as another question is asked again: Was painter Walter Sickert really Jack the Ripper? He had already been considered as a conspirator in a possible plot led by Dr. William Gull to protect the reputation of Prince Eddie.

Famed crime novelist Patricia Cornwell is convinced that all available evidence points to artist Walter Sickert (pictured) as the Ripper.

Sickert was also suspected by a few Ripperologists who noted the grim subject matter and style of his paintings. He was fascinated by crime scenes, often painted portraits of prostitutes, and used a style where, according to historian Wolf Vanderlinden, "Details [were added] using only a few strokes of the brush. . . . That makes some of his subjects' faces appear to be mutilated. . . . With Sickert . . . it is very hard to tell what might be shadow and what might be blood. . . . You see what you want to see."[82]

Crime novelist Patricia Cornwell is convinced that blood, rather than shadow, obsessed Sickert. She believes Walter Sickert was Jack the Ripper. As she has stated about Sickert's work, "Some of his paintings, if you juxtapose them with some of the [Ripper victims'] morgue photos, are extraordinarily chilling."[83] Cornwell maintains that Sickert's fascination with wounds and violence began in childhood, when he underwent painful surgeries to correct a birth defect. As a former forensic technician (as well as a new Ripperologist), Cornwell recently set out to test her theory scientifically.

Cornwell had genetic material on items Sickert used compared with fingerprints and saliva left on one Ripper letter and its stamp. While the first kind of DNA test came back negative, another kind of test matched. Cornwell claims that this match, while not totally conclusive, is strong enough to declare that Sickert was indeed the Jack the Ripper, that this great mystery is now solved, and the case is closed. This view, however, is hotly debated by scientists as well as other Ripperologists.

Scientists note that the DNA match Cornwell finally made is much less conclusive than she suggests. According to geneticist Terry Melton, "a century-old scrap of paper is [covered with] DNA from the many people who handled it, even if they deposited only a single skin cell."[84] Furthermore, other scientists observe that, on the two Sickert items that do surprisingly contain DNA from only one person, the match merely places the donor statistically with a group of several hundred thousand people. Any one of those people could have had DNA like the kind Cornwell found on the Ripper letter.

"The Naked Corpse"

Ripperologists question Cornwell's claim for other reasons. They point out that most letters supposedly sent by the Ripper are now considered frauds. The letter she tested is not one of the three or four that actually may have been penned by the Whitechapel Murderer. At best, these skeptical historians say, Cornwell's match proves only that Walter Sickert was among the many Ripper-obsessed tricksters who wrote and mailed counterfeit letters.

Ripperologists acknowledge that Sickert seems to have been fascinated by crime and criminals. This interest overlapped with his art. In a 1912 article, Sickert even wrote, "Enlarged photographs of the naked corpse should be in every art school as a standard of drawing from the nude."[85] Historians point out, though, that this interest could well explain why some of Sickert's paintings resemble morgue photographs of Ripper victims. These photographs were published in a book before Sickert painted the pictures in question. He could have bought this book and studied the photographs.

Skeptics also note that he probably painted prostitutes because they were among women in Victorian times who would willingly pose in the nude for painters. Sickert's remarks about these models indicate that he liked, rather than hated, them. In a letter to a friend, Sickert described his experience with French prostitutes who had posed for him. He wrote: "From 9 to 4, it is an uninterrupted joy, caused by these pretty, little, obliging models who laugh and unembarrassedly be themselves while posing like angels. They are glad to be here, and are not in a hurry."[86] These words do not support a view of Walter Sickert as a bloodthirsty murderer with a particular hatred of prostitutes.

Art historians have a further reason to disagree with Cornwell's claim. While she notes that the titles of some of Sickert's paintings focus on murder, death, or other grim topics, historians point out that the painter often gave each work several titles. They think Cornwell has read too much into some titles. Sickert did call one bleak painting of a naked woman in bed with a clothed man sitting beside her *The Camden Town Murder*. It may depict a murder that took place in that neighborhood. Cornwell, though, thinks this paint-

ing represents the slaughter of Mary Jane Kelly, butchered in her own bed. Yet historians point out that Sickert also called this painting *What Shall We Do for the Rent?* The picture is much less ominous with this title, which suggests that the shadowed woman is merely asleep or resting, rather than dead. Despite Patricia Cornwell's claims and use of the latest scientific tools, mysteries still surround the identity and crimes of Jack the Ripper.

Many Ripperologists question the methodology used by Patricia Cornwell in her investigation of Walter Sickert.

Mindhunting the Ripper

Another kind of modern investigative tool is also being used to hunt the Ripper. Called criminal profiling, it is not an exact science. Instead, its practitioners use evidence from a crime scene, information about the victim, and information about perpetrators of similar crimes to create a picture, or profile, of a possible suspect. This picture usually provides the suspect's probable age, appearance, personality, health, intellectual ability, family history, and work experience. It also includes the suspect's probable relationship to the victims and knowledge of the crime scene. Police then use this profile to narrow down the field of suspects to only one or two.

Criminal profilers are usually called in on cases of violent, repeated, or unusual crime. They have successfully helped police capture murderers, rapists, arsonists, bombers, kidnappers, and terrorists. Profiler John Douglas terms the work he does "mindhunting." In 1988, during the centennial of the Whitechapel murders, Douglas was asked by producers of a television documentary to mindhunt the mysteriously elusive Ripper.

Douglas developed a clear and thorough portrait of Jack the Ripper. According to Douglas, this serial killer was undoubtedly

> an asocial loner. Dress neat and orderly. Employment in positions where he could work alone and experience vicariously his destructive fantasies, perhaps as a butcher or hospital or mortuary attendant. Sexual relationships mostly with prostitutes. May have contracted venereal disease. Aged in his late twenties. Employed since the murders were mostly at the weekends. Free from family accountability and so unlikely to have been married. Not surgically skilled. Probably in some form of trouble with the police before the first murder. Lived or worked in the Whitechapel area and his first homicide would have

been close to his home or place of work. Undoubtedly the police would have interviewed him. [87]

After combining this profile with witness descriptions of the Ripper, Douglas concluded that the killer was madman David Cohen or someone very like him.

Signature of a Killer

Professional profilers are well aware of the limits of their technique. Often, they are able to draw a clear composite picture of the criminal, but several individuals may fit this composite. For example, Ripperologist Bruce Paley maintains that Douglas's picture actually best describes suspect Joseph Barnett, who had lived with victim Mary Jane Kelly. Paley is convinced that the monstrous mutilation of Kelly's face is

A doctor's on-the-spot sketch of victim Catherine Eddowes shows that her body was cut open. Such diabolical "surgery" may have been a crime signature of the Ripper.

George Hutchinson (right), who reported seeing Mary Jane Kelly walking with the Ripper, is, himself, a suspect in the murders.

further proof of Barnett's guilt. According to Paley, this mutilation satisfied an emotional need in Kelly's frustrated lover that her murder alone could not. Profilers call such deeds the signature of a killer. Yet, as with much surrounding the mysterious Ripper, this signature is not easily read and remains controversial.

Profiler James Cook finds a different signature in the Whitechapel murders. This psychologist thinks the removal of body parts, specifically sexual organs, provided the emotional outlet the Ripper needed. Using Cook's profile, along with physical descriptions by witnesses, Ripperologist John Eddleston has identified supposed witness George Hutchinson as the most likely killer. Eddleston says that Hutchinson cast suspicion upon himself through his unbelieveably detailed account of the man he supposedly saw with Mary Jane Kelly that fatal morning. A casual encounter, late at night on a dimly lit street, would not have yielded so much specific information. Hutchinson, who knew Kelly well enough that she tried to borrow money from him, reported:

> A man tapped [Kelly] on the shoulder and said something to her. They both burst out laughing. I heard her say "Alright" to him and the man said "You will be alright for what I have told you." He then placed his right hand around her shoulders. He also had a kind of small parcel in his left hand, with a kind of strap round it. . . . They both then came past . . . and the man hung down his head with his hat over his eyes. I stooped down and looked him in the face. He looked at me stern. They both went into Dorset Street. I followed them. They both stood at the corner . . . for about 3 minutes. He said something to her. She said, "Alright my dear, come along, you will be comfortable." He then placed his arm around her shoulder and gave her a kiss. She said she had lost her handkerchief. He then pulled his handkerchief, a red one, out and gave it to her. They both then went up the court[yard] together. . . . I stood there . . . to see if they came out. They did not so I went away.[88]

Hutchinson also provided a detailed physical description of this man, even mentioning that he had dark eyes and eyelashes. It is this level of detail that Eddleston finds incredible.

Eddleston also finds it suspicious that Hutchinson only stepped forward with this elaborate account after he feared exposure. Newspapers had published a witness's description of someone resembling Hutchinson talking with Kelly that last night. Eddleston also finds it significant that Hutchinson does not apear in the London census taken in 1891, and there are no records of where he subsequently lived. If George Hutchinson's later location could be determined, Eddleston wonders if there also would be reports of Ripper-like slayings in that area.

While Eddleston does not declare absolutely that George Hutchinson was the Ripper, he does believe that Hutchinson—among all the suspects to date—most closely matches the Whitechapel Murderer's profile. This kind of approximate match is the best that modern investigative techniques and science have been able to provide in this mysterious case.

Time Reveals All?

Did Jack the Ripper leave a cunning clue to his hidden identity? Those who believe James Maybrick was the Ripper like to point to his family crest. They believe its motto, Time Reveals All, chosen by Maybrick himself, predicted the unmasking of its author as the mysterious Ripper. Yet many people would disagree with this saying, believing the true identity of the Whitechapel Murderer may never be revealed.

For most people actively involved with this case, the crimes were never satisfactorily solved. Assistant Police Commissioner McNaughten kept a reminder of this painful failure in front of him. A photograph of the mutilated remains of Mary Jane Kelly stood on his desk for many years. Today, while the hunt for the Ripper goes on, some historians believe it may be impossible to find conclusive, irrefutable proof about any suspect. Such undeniable proof would have to be based on a series of amazing coincidences. For example, Ripperologist Michael Gordon believes Severin Klosowski (also known as George Chapman) was the Ripper. Yet Gordon admits that Klosowski could be proven guilty only if investigators discovered a mutilated woman's body and bloody knife walled up in one of Klosowski's shops, a confession written by Klosowski, and a descendent of Klosowski for a successful matching of family DNA with DNA left on this new evidence. Gordon ruefully notes how unlikely it is that this set of coincidences will ever occur.

Even though they realize the odds against them, Ripper-ologists enthusiastically continue their hunt. The mysteries of these unsolved crimes and their unknown perpetrator are too compelling for these dedicated hunters to stop their search. Historian Donald Rumbelow admits that "I have

A movie scene shows the Ripper about to mutilate his victim. The identity of the killer continues to mystify investigators of the case.

always had the feeling that on the Day of Judgment, when all things shall be known, when I and other generations of Ripperologists ask for Jack the Ripper to step forward and call out his true name, we shall turn and look with blank astonishment at one another as he does so and say 'Who?'"[89] Rumbelow's view fits in with those of criminal profilers. These investigative professionals know that their profiles may well match a citizen of grim Whitechapel who has yet to come to the attention of any historian.

Some of the books written about Jack the Ripper claim to have solved the mystery of his identity. Yet the debate about the real identity of this brutal serial killer goes on, fascinating young and old, newcomers and veteran Ripperologists alike. The passage of time only seems to increase the many mysteries that surround that monstrous figure of evil, terrible Jack the Ripper.

Notes

Introduction: A Case That Haunts Us

1. Quoted in Donald Rumbelow, *Jack the Ripper: The Complete Casebook.* Chicago: Contemporary Books, 1988, p. 180.
2. Rumbelow, *Jack the Ripper*, p. 3.
3. Philip Sugden, *The Complete History of Jack the Ripper.* New York: Carroll and Graf, 1995, p. 1.
4. Sugden, *The Complete History of Jack the Ripper*, p. 3.
5. Sugden, *The Complete History of Jack the Ripper*, p. 7.

Chapter 1: Autumn of Terror

6. Quoted in Rumbelow, *Jack the Ripper*, p. 18.
7. Quoted in Rumbelow, *Jack the Ripper*, p. 20.
8. Quoted in Rumbelow, *Jack the Ripper*, p. 20.
9. Quoted in Stephen P. Ryder and John A. Piper, *Casebook: Jack the Ripper.* www.casebook.org.
10. Quoted in Paul Begg, *Jack the Ripper: The Definitive History.* London: Pearson Education, 2003, p. 87.
11. Quoted in M.J. Trow, *The Many Faces of Jack the Ripper.* Chicester, Great Britain: Summersdale Publishers, 1997, p. 46.
12. Quoted in Stewart P. Evans and Keith Skinner, eds., *The Ultimate Jack the Ripper Companion: An Illustrated Encyclopedia.* New York: Carroll and Graf, 2001, p. 29.
13. Quoted in Begg, *Jack the Ripper: The Definitive History*, p. 150.
14. Quoted in Evans and Skinner, *The Ultimate Jack the Ripper Companion*, pp. 97–98.
15. Quoted in Begg, *Jack the Ripper: The Definitive History*, p. 155.
16. L. Perry Curtis, *Jack the Ripper and the London Press.* New Haven, CT: Yale University Press, 2001, p. 16.
17. Quoted in John J. Eddleston, *Jack the Ripper: An Encyclopedia.* Santa Barbara, CA: ABC-CLIO, 2001, p. 156.
18. Quoted in Eddleston, *Jack the Ripper*, p. 157.
19. Quoted in Sugden, *The Complete History of Jack the Ripper*, p. 171.
20. Quoted in Sugden, *The Complete History of Jack the Ripper*, p. 197.
21. Quoted in Terence Sharkey, *Jack the Ripper: One Hundred Years of Investigation.* London: Ward Lock, 1987, p. 43.
22. Quoted in Sugden, *The Complete History of Jack the Ripper*, p. 236.
23. Quoted in Evans and Skinner, *The Ultimate Jack the Ripper Companion*, p. 228.
24. Quoted in Evans and Skinner, *The Ultimate Jack the Ripper Companion*, p. 231.
25. Quoted in Begg, *Jack the Ripper: The Definitive History*, p. 197.
26. Quoted in Eddleston, *Jack the Ripper*, p. 262.

27. Quoted in Eddleston, *Jack the Ripper*, pp. 160–62.

Chapter 2: "Oh, Murder!"

28. Quoted in Trow, *The Many Faces of Jack the Ripper*, p. 58.
29. Quoted in Sugden, *The Complete History of Jack the Ripper*, p. 316.
30. Quoted in Sharkey, *Jack the Ripper*, p. 79.
31. Quoted in Sugden, *The Complete History of Jack the Ripper*, p. 278.
32. Quoted in Martin Jakubowski and Nathan Braund, eds., *The Mammoth Book of Jack the Ripper*. New York: Carroll and Graf, 1999, p. 15.
33. Quoted in Sugden, *The Complete History of Jack the Ripper*, p. 289.
34. Quoted in Evans and Skinner, *The Ultimate Jack the Ripper Companion*, p. 149.
35. Quoted in Sugden, *The Complete History of Jack the Ripper*, p. 291.
36. Quoted in Sharkey, *Jack the Ripper*, p. 54.
37. Quoted in Rumbelow, *Jack the Ripper*, p. 72.
38. Quoted in Evans and Skinner, *The Ultimate Jack the Ripper Companion*, p. 126.
39. Quoted in Rumbelow, *Jack the Ripper*, p. 120.
40. Quoted in Sharkey, *Jack the Ripper*, p. 67.
41. Quoted in Sharkey, *Jack the Ripper*, p. 66.
42. Quoted in Evans and Skinner, *The Ultimate Jack the Ripper Companion*, p. 397.
43. Quoted in Sharkey, *Jack the Ripper*, p. 70.
44. Quoted in Sharkey, *Jack the Ripper*, p. 76.
45. Quoted in Sugden, *The Complete History of Jack the Ripper*, p. 282.

Chapter 3: Was the Ripper Mad or Sane?

46. Quoted in Begg, *Jack the Ripper: The Definitive History*, p. 157.
47. Quoted in Melvin Harris, *The True Face of Jack the Ripper*. London: O'Mara, 1994, p. 24.
48. Quoted in Begg, *Jack the Ripper: The Definitive History*, pp. 267–68.
49. Quoted in Begg, *Jack the Ripper: The Definitive History*, pp. 257–58.
50. Quoted in Jakubowski and Braund, eds., *The Mammoth Book of Jack the Ripper*, p. 176.
51. Quoted in Begg, *Jack the Ripper: The Definitive History*, pp. 257–58.
52. Quoted in Sharkey, *Jack the Ripper*, p. 119.
53. Quoted in Begg, *Jack the Ripper: The Definitive History*, pp. 257–58.
54. Quoted in Paul Begg, *Jack the Ripper: The Uncensored Facts*. London: Robson Books, 1988, p. 61.
55. Quoted in Begg, *Jack the Ripper: The Definitive History*, p. 264.
56. Stephen Knight, *Jack the Ripper: The Final Solution*. London: George G. Harrap, 1976, p. 13.
57. Quoted in Knight, *Jack the Ripper*, p. 253.
58. Quoted in Sugden, *The Complete History of Jack the Ripper*, p. 118.
59. Sugden, *The Complete History of Jack the Ripper*, p. 118.

Chapter 4: Was His Motive Hatred or Love?

60. Quoted in Eddleston, *Jack the Ripper*, p. 237.
61. Quoted in Ryder and Piper, *Casebook*.
62. Quoted in Sharkey, *Jack the Ripper*, p. 129.

63. John Douglas and Mark Olshaker, *The Cases That Haunt Us: From Jack the Ripper to Jon Benet Ramsey.* New York: Scribner, 2000, p. 71.

64. Quoted in R. Michael Gordon, *Alias Jack the Ripper: Beyond the Usual Whitechapel Suspects.* Jefferson, NC: McFarland, 2001, p. 312.

65. Quoted in Sugden, *The Complete History of Jack the Ripper,* p. 453.

66. Quoted in Ryder and Piper, *Casebook.*

67. Quoted in Ryder and Piper, *Casebook.*

68. Quoted in Ryder and Piper, *Casebook.*

69. Quoted in Ryder and Piper, *Casebook.*

70. Quoted in Jakubowski and Braund, eds., *The Mammoth Book of Jack the Ripper,* p. 237.

71. Quoted in Jakubowski and Braund, eds., *The Mammoth Book of Jack the Ripper,* p. 237.

72. Quoted in Jakubowski and Braund, eds., *The Mammoth Book of Jack the Ripper,* p. 242.

73. Quoted in Daniel Farson, *Jack the Ripper.* London: Michael Joseph, 1972, p. 98.

74. Quoted in Evans and Skinner, *The Ultimate Jack the Ripper Companion,* p. 467.

Chapter 5: Does Science Have the Answer?

75. Rumbelow, *Jack the Ripper,* p. 132.

76. Quoted in Shirley Harrison, *The Diary of Jack the Ripper: The Discovery, the Investigation, the Debate.* New York: Hyperion, 1993, p. 271.

77. Quoted in Harrison, *The Diary of Jack the Ripper,* p. 273.

78. Quoted in Harrison, *The Diary of Jack the Ripper,* p. 288.

79. Quoted in Harrison, *The Diary of Jack the Ripper,* p. 292.

80. Quoted in Harris, *The True Face of Jack the Ripper,* p. 189.

81. Quoted in Harris, *The True Face of Jack the Ripper,* p. 188.

82. Quoted in Ryder and Piper, *Casebook.*

83. Quoted in Ryder and Piper, *Casebook.*

84. Terry Melton, "Neither History nor Science," *The Scientist,* February 10, 2003. www.the-scientist.com.

85. Quoted in Patricia Cornwell, *Portrait of a Killer: Jack the Ripper—Case Closed.* New York: G.P. Putnam's Sons, 2002, p. 73.

86. Quoted in Ryder and Piper, *Casebook.*

87. Quoted in Eddleston, *Jack the Ripper,* p. 154.

88. Quoted in Eddleston, *Jack the Ripper,* pp. 279–80.

89. Rumbelow, *Jack the Ripper,* p. 41.

For Further Reading

Books: Nonfiction

Stewart P. Evans and Keith Skinner, eds., *Jack the Ripper and the Whitechapel Murders*. London: Public Record Office, 2002. A collection of facsimiles of documents kept in the British National Archive. Readers can handle letters, handwritten police reports, and coroners' notes that recreate the originals in size, color, and texture. A pamphlet explains the significance of each document.

Martin Jakubowski and Nathan Braund, eds., *The Mammoth Book of Jack the Ripper*. New York: Carroll and Graf, 1999. A thorough introduction to the facts of the case, this book also contains essays by sixteen authors explaining their own views about the Ripper's identity.

M.J. Trow, *The Many Faces of Jack the Ripper*. Chicester, Great Britain: Summersdale Publishers, 1997. A well-illustrated introduction to the background, facts, and theories about the Ripper case, including photographs of modern London.

Camille Wolff, ed., *Who Was Jack the Ripper? A Collection of Present-Day Theories and Observations*. London: Grey House Books, 1995. This collection of fifty-three short essays is a thorough and entertaining look at the many ideas today about the Ripper.

Book: Fiction

Robert Bloch, "Yours Truly, Jack the Ripper." In *The Best of Robert Bloch*, ed. Lester del Rey. New York: Ballantine Books, 1977. This fictional short story, written in the 1940s, captures the mystery and terror surrounding the case.

Website

Steven P. Ryder and John A. Piper, *Casebook: Jack the Ripper* (www.casebook.org). This website provides an excellent, detailed introduction to the facts and controversies of the case. It includes newspaper articles from the Ripper era and is regularly updated.

Works Consulted

Books

Paul Begg, *Jack the Ripper: The Definitive History.* London: Pearson Education, 2003. This extensive, illustrated history of the case also explains how London's East End became home to the city's poorest citizens.

———, *Jack the Ripper: The Uncensored Facts.* London: Robson Books, 1988. Begg's first book on the subject is a thorough introduction to the case and current up to its 1988 publication date.

Patricia Cornwell, *Portrait of a Killer: Jack the Ripper—Case Closed.* New York: G.P. Putnam's Sons, 2002. Argues that painter Walter Sickert was Jack the Ripper.

L. Perry Curtis, *Jack the Ripper and the London Press.* New Haven, CT: Yale University Press, 2001. Looks at the ways in which newspapers in the 1880s and 1890s presented the case to readers.

John Douglas and Mark Olshaker, *The Cases That Haunt Us: From Jack the Ripper to Jon Benet Ramsey.* New York: Scribner, 2000. Cowritten by a former FBI profiler of criminals, this book includes a chapter detailing the Ripper's probable background and personality.

John J. Eddleston, *Jack the Ripper: An Encyclopedia.* Santa Barbara, CA: ABC-CLIO, 2001. This thorough reference work lists all suspects and describes Ripper-related books, films, and television episodes.

Stewart P. Evans and Keith Skinner, eds., *The Ultimate Jack the Ripper Companion: An Illustrated Encyclopedia.* New York: Carroll and Graf, 2001. A useful collection of all the official documents and major newspaper reports about the case.

Daniel Farson, *Jack the Ripper.* London: Michael Joseph, 1972. The author, who believes M.J. Druitt was the Ripper, presents material that was known up to this book's date of publication.

R. Michael Gordon, *Alias Jack the Ripper: Beyond the Usual Whitechapel Suspects.* Jefferson, NC: McFarland, 2001. Maintains that Severin Klosowski (also known as George Chapman) was the Ripper.

Melvin Harris, *The True Face of Jack the Ripper.* London: O'Mara, 1994. Argues, unconvincingly, that Robert D'Onston Stephenson was the Ripper. The chapters on the Maybrick diary are thorough.

Shirley Harrison, *The Diary of Jack the Ripper: The Discovery, the Investigation, the Debate.* New York: Hyperion, 1993. Contends that James Maybrick was Jack the Ripper. This illustrated book also contains a facsimile copy and transcript of the Maybrick diary and three essays that debate the diary's authenticity.

Stephen Knight, *Jack the Ripper: The Final Solution.* London: George G. Harrap, 1976. The author argues that Dr. William Gull, as part of a royal conspiracy, committed the Whitechapel Murders.

Donald Rumbelow, *Jack the Ripper: The Complete Casebook.* Chicago: Contemporary Books, 1988. Written by a former London police officer, this is a thorough, illustrated history of the autumn of terror.

Terence Sharkey, *Jack the Ripper: One Hundred Years of Investigation.* London: Ward Lock, 1987. This book lists all suspects considered up to its date of publication.

Philip Sugden, *The Complete History of Jack the Ripper.* New York: Carroll and Graf, 1995. This book is a thorough, excellent history of the case. The author is balanced in his presentation of possible suspects, suggesting that George Chapman might have been the Ripper.

Periodical

Terry Melton, "Neither History nor Science," *The Scientist,* Feruary 10, 2003. www.the-scientist.com.

Index

Picture Credits

About the Author

Natalie M. Rosinsky earned her doctor of philosophy degree in English from the University of Wisconsin-Madison. Before becoming a professional writer, she was a high school teacher, a college professor, and a corporate trainer and instructional designer. She has written more than seventy articles and books for children and young adults. She and her husband, Donald F. Larsson, live in Mankato, Minnesota, with their son, Daniel.